D0088834

BRIDGE OF THE SINGLE HAIR

BRIDGE OF THE SINGLE HAIR

CANDIDA PUGH

LANGDON STREET PRESS

Copyright © 2011 by Candida Pugh.

Langdon Street Press
212 3rd Avenue North, Suite 290
Minneapolis, MN 55401
612.455.2293
www.langdonstreetpress.com

All rights reserved. No part of this publication may be
reproduced, stored in a retrieval system, or transmitted, in any
form or by any means, electronic, mechanical, photocopying,
recording, or otherwise, without the prior written permission of
the author.

ISBN-13: 978-1-936782-28-4
LCCN: 2011928282

Distributed by Itasca Books

Cover Design by Alan Pranke
Typeset by Jill Kennedy

Printed in the United States of America

For Ellic Lee, who lived and died unannounced

1

ROSEMARY'S BOYFRIEND changed my life. I never
met him, but he changed the course of my personal history
as carelessly as a smoker scars a meadow, oblivious to any
connection between his stroll through the dry grass and the
wildfire that follows. I never knew his name. Rosemary called
him "my black boyfriend," relishing the seismic activity this
set off in people's eyes.

She and I had crap jobs in the basement of McCullough
Worthington, a huge legal chop shop for anyone with deep
pockets to protect. The temperature down there careened
between sub-zero and a steam bath, and the sole arteries
linking us to our masters above were a pneumatic tube and a
series of dumb waiters. Our orders arrived with a whoosh and
a thump. After a day of steady whooshing and thumping—
sending us repeatedly into the file room to retrieve or return
manila folders—Rosemary flung herself at the tube, shrieking,

"We're seventeen, for Christ's sake. We're too young to die of boredom!"

I liked her. She made me laugh and she often told me I was pretty, which, of course, I never believed, not least of all because of the way she would tell me: "Your eyes might be on the small side but your nose is small too and that's good. And, it could be your features only look small because your forehead's wide. So chin up, girl, because all the parts go together pretty good."

"Think I should cancel my audition with MGM?"

"C'mon, Jeri, you know you're a fine looking woman. So go already! The worst they can do is turn you down," she grinned.

If Rosemary had gone on the march with me, if she'd been sitting next to me in the church, things would've turned out different. Rosemary never permitted anyone to be serious about anything. She'd tickle you if you tried not to laugh. But instead of keeping our date, she let her boyfriend talk her into heading over to Griffith Park. "A loaf of bread, a jug of Thunderbird, and a cow," she told me two days later. "Turns out, I was the cow."

* * *

So I gave up waiting for her and went by myself. Under the noses of L.A.'s Finest, somewhere around two hundred marchers and I limped into the Sixth Street AME Zion Church. For several minutes, we did a lot of mumbling and shuffling, looking for an available place to squat. I'm fairly athletic but after two hours of dodging all those work boots and saddle shoes, I wanted a nap.

I half-dozed until the pastor boomed, "God has his eye on the sparrow!" At that point Rosemary, I'm sure, would've snorted, "That's why the planet's so fucked up. God's busy bird-watching." A few moments later I was jolted into attentiveness again when he beseeched heaven: "Remove the scales from their eyes, dear Lord, that they shall see the paths of righteousness."

"Turn left at Sanctimony and Tedium," I mouthed to my AWOL buddy. But I hadn't mouthed it, I'd spoken the words. Someone hissed, "Hush!" and somebody else clicked her tongue. A few rows ahead, a grim-faced woman turned around, seeking the offender. I pretended to look around too.

The church was big enough to hold the crowd, but just barely, and the building had seen better days. The windows, overlaid with "stained-glass" contact paper, needed a good scrubbing. There were no cushions on the wooden seats, no rug on the scarred floor. Everything was dingy and cramped. Even the pews were small. Whichever way I twisted, the hymnal rack dug into my knees. I pulled out a torn green paper fan on a stick, imprinted with HARDY FUNERAL HOME, and used it to move the humidity around. When I shifted again, I scraped my knee and winced. I blamed my mother for my long legs. T.J., my grandmother, was practically a midget.

I longed to get out of there. After all, I'd gone on the march, I'd made my statement. *God has his eye on the sparrow? Please.* I looked up and down the row. With four people on one side and five on the other, there was no escaping without ruffling a lot of feathers. Since a majority of those feathers belonged to pious black people—I saw only a scattering of white faces—I could well picture the scene if I got up, bumping into knees, muttering, "Excuse me, excuse me," until nearly every pair of brown eyes in the church glared at my white face.

The Reverend Wilcox finally took a seat in one of the high-backed chairs facing us. He looked rather disappointed, I thought. I hoped he hadn't heard my blooper. A bony, bird-beaked woman who had been pecking the air at each chant of *amen* turned to beam at him. He gave her a distracted nod, his eyes scanning the audience. I scrunched down a bit.

Next to them on the dais sat an old man, bent over his cane, his misshapen hand moving back and forth over its smooth wood. One shoulder bulged under his shiny brown suit jacket. That bulge and the worn suit jacket made me wish I could put my arm around him and tell him everything would be okay.

In one of the last two chairs, a man of about thirty sat, looking uneasy. His clothes hung off him as if he'd lost a great deal of weight recently but, judging by the distant look in his eyes, it was more likely he'd never paid any attention to what he put on.

At the pulpit, a stocky fellow with wild gray hair signaled for us to stand and then led us through several choruses of *Keep Your Eyes on the Prize*. When I was a kid, my grandmother sometimes sang protest songs to me at bedtime. Lullabies might've been more restful but T.J. was never much into tranquility. I remember her belting out, "You Got to Go Down and Join the Union!" I'm pretty sure she didn't know the melody had started life as a Negro spiritual.

When the singing was over, the stocky man said, "Now I have the pleasure to introduce to you Mr. Dasante Mitchell. Mr. Mitchell has come to us from the struggles down South and he has a great deal to share with us this afternoon. Please give him your full attention." I wondered if he was directing this last request to me.

The dark young man in baggy clothes took the podium.

> I have just come back from Monroe, North Carolina. It's hot in Monroe. You could fry an egg on the sidewalk, that's how hot it is. For Negro children,

the heat don't let up a single hour from June through September. White children get theyselves cool in the city swimming pool. Negro children has to turn a hose on each other, if they got a hose. If they don't, they are welcome to swim in one of the filthy holes around town, swimming holes where a good number of their kinfolk have perished.

He paused to give us some time to locate those drowned bodies in our minds, small brown arms and legs that would never wiggle again. Somebody gulped back a sob. A few seats away a broad-faced woman, mopping her brow with a large yellow handkerchief, met my eyes. My smile faltered when she didn't return it. She'd probably heard my wisecrack.

Everybody pays taxes in Monroe. The city fathers don't say to a colored man, "Hey, boy, y'all ain't getting the same services so it ain't right for y'all to pay the same taxes." No, sir. Doesn't happen. Negroes pay the same income tax. The same property tax. They pay the same sales tax. Taxes. Now that's one place you will see equal rights. Groceries, too, they cost the same. Clothing and shoes cost just what a white family pays. Sometimes a little more, depending on how inclined the storekeeper might be to larceny.

Knowing laughter flitted through the church but ceased as the yellow handkerchief lady pivoted on her massive bottom and hissed, "Y'all be respectful now!" I tried to imagine watching a clerk ring up my groceries for more than was stamped on them, and I tried to imagine shutting my mouth about it because, if I complained, I'd be the one in trouble.

And so it is with public transportation. A worn-out old cleaning lady has to climb up onto the front of the bus so she can pay her fare. Then she has to climb down and go to the back door to climb up again and get her a seat. But even if she does find some place to rest her bones at the back of the bus, she will have to stand on her swolled-up feet if some white man come along and shoos her out of it. Nevertheless. Nevertheless. She's going to pay the exact same fare he pays.

A cold smile dented his cheeks. Behind him on her perch, bird lady pecked vigorously. Rosemary would've done a riff on bird lady. I was starting to think it might be a good thing she hadn't shown. If the two of us had been sitting there snickering, we would've been tossed out. And now I really wanted to stay.

That is the gracious Southern way of life the Klan has sworn to uphold.

He turned so that light coming through the windows mottled his honey-colored face. I loved him for caring about that old lady. Two Saturdays before, a snotty guy in a suit had shoved T.J. out of the way when we were boarding a downtown bus. He grabbed the last seat. Before my grandmother could tell him off herself—which she certainly would have—I stomped on his foot, telling him, "Get your butt out of my grandmother's seat or I'll take out your other Buster Brown."

Two months ago a group of teenagers went over to the Monroe public pool. *Public* means that pool was part of their community and their folks had paid to build that pool, and their folks was paying still to maintain it. So those teenagers thought they might take a swim. Word went out that some nigras was getting uppity and a hundred or so upstanding white citizens ran down there, saying they was going to lynch those young 'uns. But the children would not be moved. Things got ugly and some of those teenagers got their heads busted but they would not be moved. So the city fathers shut down that swimming pool. If that pool had to serve for colored children, well, it just wasn't going to serve for anybody. That's how much they abominate integration in North Carolina.

Indiana rushed into my memory, along with the only photograph I'd ever seen of my grandmother as a little girl. The picture had faded, her face almost a blur, but her sagging dress stood out and, behind her, a stretch of barren farmland. In my head, T.J.'s Indiana childhood was all mixed up with a hot December night in L.A. She and I were walking home from the corner store. Near our apartment building, I was half-blinded by a flashing police car light. When my eyes adjusted, I saw a black kid face down on the filthy sidewalk, a cop with his boot pressing on the kid's back. When T.J. complained, the cop told her to "fuck off," and we went inside, T.J. shaking with rage. She opened a beer and began to talk about something that had happened when she was a girl, something that had haunted her all her life.

And it's not just in North Carolina. Y'all know what happened in Alabama this past May. Y'all might think I mean the very first Freedom Ride but you'd be wrong. The first Freedom Ride wasn't called a Freedom Ride, it was called a Journey of Reconciliation and it took place in the year nineteen and forty-seven. Sixteen people—eight black, eight white—took a Greyhound into Dixie. First place they got in trouble—North Carolina. What made them go on that ride was something called the *Irene*

7

Morgan Decision.

Dasante Mitchell's light eyes darkened to granite.

In the summer of 1944, Miss Morgan—feeling something sick and no doubt sick and tired—was told to get up and give her seat to a white couple on a Greyhound passing through Virginia. The young lady, who was on her way to Baltimore to consult a doctor, said no, she wasn't going to do it. And so the bus driver call in the sheriff. That peace officer try to take Miss Morgan into custody. Before he made the arrest, she kicked him in an indelicate locale. I expect she had not yet heard about nonviolent resistance.

Afterward she say she will plead guilty and pay a fine for committing an outrage on the person of the constable, which she acknowledged she had done, but she would *not* plead guilty and she would *not* pay a fine for refusing to give up the seat she had paid for. Her case went all the way up to the Supreme Court. Thurgood Marshall, a Negro, argued it and won. In a manner of speaking.

The Court did rule that whenever a bus come across a state border, the Constitution say you aren't allowed to make some people sit in back because they the wrong color. Y'all might think that's a strange thing in the law—segregation being perfectly all right inside the state but unconstitutional when it's heading into some other state. Somebody much smarter than me one time said, "The law is an ass." I don't rightly recall who that was but that particular law sure do seem the work of an ass. Yet and still, even that particular law might be just a bit less of an ass than are at least a few of the people appointed to see that it gets carried out.

I felt as if all of us in that room breathed together. Not one of us coughed or shifted in the pews. The funeral home paper fan I had been waving hung in mid-air, momentarily forgotten.

Because in nineteen and forty-seven, as in nineteen and sixty-one, no one defended the right of a Negro to do what was legal to do. No officer of the law. No, sir. The Negroes that stood up for what was right have been the only ones obeying the law of the land. The only ones.

The old man on the dais closed his eyes. Bird lady placed a claw on his humped shoulder, her expression soft.

This past May Freedom Riders set out once again for Dixie. When the bus carrying the first group of Freedom Riders reached Anniston, Alabama, the Klan was there—hiding, as befits the Klan. When that bus roll into the depot, those good old boys jump out of their hidey-holes and went at it with iron pipes. They slash its tires and smash its windows. They cave in its sides. They want to get on to bust some heads but the driver would not open the door. The local police is standing by, and they just watch. So that bus driver decide to get that bus out of there, but by the time he get a couple miles away, those flat tires made him to pull over. And now here come the Klan. One of those righteous white men throws a firebomb in through a broken window. Then they pin the doors shut with the Freedom Riders trapped inside. Those courageous freedom fighters would've been burnt alive but for one thing: The gas tank

exploded. The Klan ran away like chaff flying out
of a thresher. Klan cowardice saved those lives.

He paused and raked his gaze across the faces of his audience.
The yellow handkerchief lady dabbed her eyes and when I
looked over at her, she gave me a half-smile, maybe because
my eyes were spilling over too.

Y'all need to remember that. The segregationists
will run away. They will flee our sword of justice—
each and every time y'all stand up to them. Might
be they can bend us but they won't never break us.
And, in the end, the Klan and all who believe as they
believe will bow down before our cause. Brothers
and sisters, heed my words: We *shall* overcome. *We
shall overcome*. Because we shall *not* be moved!

We leapt to our feet, shouting, our fists pumping the air:

Segregation, it shall be removed!
Segregation, it shall be removed!
Just like the garbage standing in the water,
It shall be removed!

Dasante Mitchell waited for us to settle down. He seemed
to be listening to something we couldn't hear, but when he
looked up, I felt his eyes on me. He spoke directly to me.

We need bodies. Hundreds of bodies. We need them
to fill those jails. We need them to empty out their
coffers. We need bodies to drain the poison of their
corruption. Hear me: We need bodies to seize this
victory. And I tell you today we will be victorious.
Nothing will turn us around. Nothing. Segregation
is on its deathbed.

A wise man once said that all it takes for evil to

triumph, brothers and sisters, is for good men to do nothing. With Freedom Riders inside that bus, their lungs burning up and their lives in sorest danger, our nation's highest officer of the law did—nothing.

He slammed his fist on the podium and I felt my pulse throbbing in my arms and legs. It was difficult to sit still. I wanted to shout, to yell at those politicians in Washington, to make them see how wrong they were to act like injustice wasn't their job to stop.

Don't y'all be those good people who do nothing in the face of such wickedness. Y'all must not continue to endure what should never be endured. Y'all must not stand by and watch. Because, my brothers and sisters, if y'all won't do it, ain't nobody gonna fight for justice.

I saw people clapping but I couldn't hear them over the roar in my head. I thought, *this must be the way it feels to take your vows as a nun or to walk over hot coals without flinching.* A hand reached down and pulled me onto the dais. Dasante Mitchell smiled.

"Thank you, sister," he said. "Thank you for heeding the call."

2

THAT EVENING I put together a meatloaf the way my grandmother liked it—half onion, half tomato sauce, with a pound or two of salt and pepper. And I oiled the skins of the Russets before roasting them so they would be crisp as November Winesaps. T.J. loved crunchy potato skins. When she hobbled in from her long day of overtime, I was slicing the green beans and the oven was playing bubbling-fat music.

"Oho," she said with a craggy smile. "Somebody's buttering me up."

"Just the potato skins."

"Perhaps you ought to cook dinner more often, if you want to slip something by me. What's up?" She took a bottle of beer from the refrigerator and slumped into the captain's chair at the head of the table. "C'mon. What's going on, Jeri?"

I dumped the green beans into a pot, turned up the flame, and sat down. "It's nothing. I mean, I'm not trying to get anything by you. I just hoped we'd have a nice dinner. It's been a long week for you."

"Hells bells, what do I have to do on a Saturday that's more fun than fighting a broken down printing press?" She took a slug of beer and peered at me. "And?"

I went over and covered the beans. "I volunteered today."

"For what?"

"The Freedom Rides."

Reaching out with knobby ink-stained fingers, she drew the newspaper across the table toward herself. "Is that so?" she said, starting to read. Her deformed hands rested on either side of the paper. She wore cheap flashy rings and I remembered her telling a friend that for many years she wouldn't wear rings or bracelets because she didn't want to call attention to her arthritic knuckles. "But then I realized something," she'd said. "I figured out rings and bracelets call attention to themselves. They take attention *away* from my hands."

"It *is* so." I turned down the flame on the beans. "I volunteered."

"Smells like that meatloaf's about done," she said without looking up.

We ate in silence, T.J. leafing through the newspaper she never had time for in the morning before she went off to her lithographer's job at six. She was justifiably, I thought, proud of being one of the few women to crack that union. Standing less than five feet tall, she nonetheless held her own with the men, hefting massive boxes of paper and tinkering with the mechanics of a balky multi-ton offset press. Although she had no talent for engineering, fear and pride kept her at it until she completed each job, mostly on time. Having stood all day on legs roped by varicose veins, she eased the pain every evening by drinking several beers. Still, I'd never seen her drunk.

"What about the Indians?"

I was staring out the kitchen window at a street lamp that

had been flickering for at least a month. "Huh?"

"I said what about the Indians."

"What *about* the Indians?"

"Aren't you going to do something about the Indians?"

"What Indians?"

"The American Indians. Been cooped up on reservations, had their land stolen, had their kids kidnapped and put in Indian school a thousand miles away. Those kids got beat up for speaking Indian. What about them?"

"I hadn't planned on doing anything about Sacco and Vanzetti either, T.J. And there's no such language as Indian."

"Don't get smart with me, young lady."

I stood up.

"Where you going?"

"I'm going to wash the dishes. And then I'm going to bed."

"It's only seven o'clock. You sick or something?"

"No, I'm not sick or something. I'm just going to bed."

"Well." She drummed on the table with her stubby nails. After a moment, she got up and turned off the water I'd been running to fill the sink. "Listen to me, Jeri. You're still underage. I could stop you."

I turned and met her eyes. "But you won't." I turned the water back on.

She sank back down at the table and resumed drumming. I went over to wipe the oilcloth. The newspaper was neatly stacked. I noticed that because T.J. is normally the world's least tidy person.

I picked up the stack. "Through with this?"

"Huh? Oh, yeah. Yeah."

I stuffed the paper into the garbage and finished wrapping up the meatloaf.

"That was good, Jeri," she said. "A good dinner. Thank you."

* * *

On Sunday I stayed in bed, pulling apart Oreos and drinking soda. T.J. knocked in the morning. I called out, "I'm reading," and she went away. In the evening she knocked again and I said, "I'm not hungry." She told me through the door that she was going out.

Half-empty bottles of flat root beer covered the nightstand. I'd stacked the cookies into towers, re-reading a deciduous copy of *Red Badge of Courage* and wondering which Henry Fleming I would turn into if they set fire to a bus I rode. When I'd had enough of that, I rolled onto my side, pulled my knees into my chest, and dozed.

Molly Whuppie skipped into my dreams. My hero when I was a child, Molly rescues her three sisters from an evil giant. I listened to her story on my 78-rpm record so many times, the record grew scratchy. Rita—which was what T.J. and I called my mother—smashed it during one of her spells. I'd bawled and kicked the wall until T.J. took me out for ice cream and told me Rita would be going back into the hospital.

Half-awake, in my head I replayed the breathless narrator's voice: "And he ran and she ran and he ran and she ran and they both ran . . . until at last they came to the bridge of the single hair and Molly Whuppie ran across but the giant could not. . ."

At two in the morning I heard T.J. locking the door of the flat and considerately padding barefoot past my bedroom. But she must've spotted my light because again she knocked, and this time she opened the door.

"You awake?"

I lay on my side, my teeth gritty with cookie flecks, *Red Badge of Courage* face down on the floor.

"I need to ask you something," she said. I just hoped she wouldn't bring up the Indians again. "Can I sit down?"

15

I nodded and she plopped onto the bed.

"Have a good night?"

"Mmm hmm. Jeri?"

"Yes?"

"Have you thought this through? I mean, have you thought about what this will mean?"

"What will it mean?"

The corners of her mouth drew down. "What about college? I thought you were going to college."

"What made you think that?"

"Your grades were always so good—"

I pulled myself up and stuck two pillows behind my back. "There's no money."

"Lots of people work their way through, missy."

"Yeah, well, I suppose they have some idea of what they want to do with their education."

"I thought you wanted to be a doctor."

"What're you talking about? When I was five?" I scrambled to my feet. "T.J., I'm going to do this. I have to do this. Frankly, I hoped you'd be proud of me. I really thought you would."

"You did not."

"Okay. I didn't. But why can't you? Won't I be fighting for things you believe in—?"

"Maybe you haven't noticed, Jeri, but we don't have much in the way of justice and equal rights here in L.A., either. Of course, that wouldn't be as exciting as going two thousand miles away to wave your mighty sword around."

"Oh, brother."

"Well, it sure seems awful spur-of-the-moment."

"It's not," I lied.

"Okay. Just tell me this: How will integrating bus stations change things for colored people? Most of them don't have the money to take a bus across state lines anyway."

"You have a better idea?"

"Jobs. That's what Negroes need. Good jobs and good wages."

"You're kidding."

She squinted hard at me. "You do know how important jobs are, right? This isn't just about you wanting to get away from that basement and have a little adventure?"

I ran my fingers through my chopped hair. "You don't get it."

"I get it, all right. You signed up because somebody spoke some mumbo jumbo and you got swept away."

I huffed, "You think Negroes need good jobs? Fine. But I don't see you lifting a finger—why don't *you* do something for a change?"

She closed her eyes. "You've got a smart mouth on you, Jeri Turner."

"Yeah, and I know where I got it."

"I've done things," she muttered. "I've done plenty of things you know nothing about."

I sat next to her and put my arm around her shoulders. She stiffened. T.J. never liked to be touched. "That was a bad thing to say—and it's wrong. I'm sorry I lost my temper. I know about the stuff from the fifties, McCarthy and HUAC, and you're the bravest woman I ever knew. It had to be awful scary when you risked losing your job, when you had me and Rita to look after. You're a good person." She sniffed, as if rejecting the compliment, but I felt her body soften. "But, T.J., please—give me a break. I want to be like that, to stand up for what's right the way you have. And I want you to be on my side."

"Damn it to hell, I should never have told you that story."

"I hope you're not thinking if something happens to me, it's going to be your fault because you told me."

"If something happens to you, it doesn't matter whose fault it is."

"Okay. But, just so you know, your story has nothing to do with me going." I reached into the drawer of my nightstand and drew out a slip of paper. "Will you sign this for me?"

T.J. scanned it. "This says you're eighteen."

"I know what it says."

She shook her head, but she held out her hand for the pen. After she signed it, she dropped the piece of paper in my lap as if she didn't want any more to do with it. She stood up and looked down at me grimly. "You're Rita's child so I can't tell you one damned thing."

I got up and kissed her lined cheek. "No, T.J. I'm *your* granddaughter. And that's the reason you can't tell me one damned thing."

3

ROOM B of the Sixth Street church held a heavy wooden table, some chairs, and not much else. The walls were decorated with crayoned Jesuses—scraggly beards and long washboard faces. Some of the Sunday school kids had used a single crayon to color both Jesus's beard and his complexion. The result looked something like the Hunchback of Notre Dame.

Two black women and two white guys were in the room when I got there, a bit late. One of the white guys introduced himself as Paul Warren, our organizer from the Congress of Racial Equality. He was probably about twenty-three or -four. He blinked so much, I wondered whether he had recently gotten contact lenses, but I decided it was nerves. T.J. must've been his barber just as she'd been mine all my life, because cowlicks of different lengths jutted out of his scalp. While we waited for the last two volunteers, he paced the tight space at the end of the room, his thumbs hooked through the belt loops of his jeans.

When the last two Freedom Riders showed up, Paul launched into his speech. I only half-listened. It had all been said at the church, I was sure. For a while, I studied the faces of the other Freedom Riders. Except for one, they looked older than me, but none of them looked more than thirty.

I checked my cuticles, wondered what Rosemary would be doing later, and mentally added up my small savings and the last paycheck I'd be getting on Friday. I thought I should give the money to T.J., just keep a few dollars for myself. I wasn't going to need much until I came home. Maybe I could talk her into using it for the appointment with the doctor she was supposed to make.

Paul was winding down. "We'll spend this week practicing techniques for dealing with violence. But tonight I'd like you to introduce yourselves and say a few words about why you're here." He jingled the change in his pocket. "Dorothy, why don't you start?"

Her hair had been crimped into a small bun tacked to the nape of her neck. Dorothy's best feature was her eyes, almost yellow, unsettling in her cocoa brown face. "I'm an opera singer," she said with a flash of those catlike eyes, as if she feared one of us might deny it.

Paul stood at the window, his back to us. "How did you come to volunteer?" he said to the garbage cans outside.

She said, "I know somebody who was on the burning bus."

Snapshots of the bus flipped through my mind. I tried to imagine myself inside it. Was I screaming? I shuddered. *Maybe I was being a fool, just like Rosemary and T.J. said. Maybe I couldn't do this.*

Dorothy touched her hair. I couldn't read her expression. "My husband's down there already," she said. I thought she sounded unhappy, but not scared.

I told myself again that the difference between a coward and a brave man was the brave man only dies once. *Yeah*, Rosemary retorted, *but that's just because the brave man doesn't have any imagination.*

I heard Paul say, "Do they call you Tommie?" He was speaking to an elfin girl in half-glasses.

"Not if I can help it, they don't. My name is Thomasine." She was the only Freedom Rider close to my age, or at least she looked it. The frizzy halo of her hair—the first Afro I ever saw—sparked like black lightning where the sun touched it.

Paul said, "Please tell me you're older than thirteen." I wondered if he was trying to flirt with her.

Thomasine said curtly, "I'm nineteen."

Paul let out a nervous giggle and turned back to the view. I suspected he imagined staring into the distance made him seem imperial. Of course, since he stood two feet from a row of trash cans, there wasn't a great deal of distance for him to stare into.

"Well, you know." Thomasine shrugged. "I graduated high school and a lot of my friends been talking about the Freedom Rides."

"But what made you sign up?"

She looked hopefully toward the door. I thought she might be considering how much she'd like to walk through it. But something changed in her face. "Any of you ever hear of Emmett Till?"

A cute blond guy with startling blue eyes said, "Of course." The other white guy, skinny and hunched, said, "You talking about that kid that was lynched a few years ago?" The skinny guy had been biting his nails ever since I came in. He probably wasn't too relaxed with the burning bus either.

Thomasine twisted a large ring. "Emmett was fourteen. They said he whistled at a white lady." She spoke in almost a sing-song voice. It sounded like reciting. I guess she was trying to keep herself from hearing what she was saying. "They put out his eye. They put out all his teeth except for two. They did things to him for hours and hours and, when they finished, they threw him in the river with something around his neck." She took in a long draught of air and focused on the ring. It didn't help me that she'd rushed through these facts. Emmett Till's mangled face was as vivid in my mind as it had been on the first day the paper published his photograph. "Emmett was sort of a half-cousin of mine. My mama went out there to be with his family at the funeral. His mama made them keep the coffin open. She didn't want anybody covering up what they did to that little boy." She pressed her lips together then and fell silent.

Paul waited, as if he hoped she might change the subject and say something to lift the gloom that had settled over us. But Thomasine was through talking. "Thank you," he said finally, and turned to me. "Your name's Geraldine?"

I dragged my eyes away from her sad face, reflecting that only moments before she'd seemed cheerful. "I go by Jeri."

"So what brings you into the Movement?"

I'd been dreading having to answer this question from the moment he put it to Dorothy. Even though Dasante Mitchell's speech inspired me to stand up when I did, I couldn't admit that. Paul might believe I was as rash as T.J. said I was. Of course, I could have talked about Emmett Till. When he was murdered, I was only two years younger than he was and I felt that if the grownups in Mississippi could kill a small boy, they could kill me. But, if I went back to his story, I'd only look like I was copying Thomasine and Paul would start thinking I didn't have any good reason to be in that room. T.J.'s story had been on my mind since the rally at the church, but I couldn't talk about it. I wasn't ever going to tell anybody that story.

So I started feeling my way into an answer: "My grandmother was a Red back in the fifties—"

Paul turned and looked at me sharply. "Your grandmother's a Communist?"

"Not anymore. The Party threw her out. T.J.'s never been much of a follower."

He crossed his arms and leaned back against the wall under a particularly grotesque Jesus. "You understand CORE doesn't take Reds, right? You don't have any affiliations with leftist groups yourself, do you?"

"I've never been much of a follower either."

"Oh?" His brows went up and I saw my mistake.

"Don't worry, I can follow if I have to."

"If you go on the Rides, you'll have to." He dismissed me, gesturing to the skinny guy. "Ned?"

"I wasn't saying I volunteered because my grandmother used to be a Communist. That would be silly."

He turned back toward me. "I'm sorry. You weren't finished?"

"I only meant she talked to me about prejudice and Negroes. Because that's one of the things the Communists I used to know worry about."

His gaze held mine for a moment. It wasn't friendly. "So is that it?"

"Not really. I wanted to say something about a fairy tale. Yeah, I know, it's really immature to talk about a kid's book. But this one meant a lot to me. It's about a little girl, Molly Whuppie." Ned snickered. "Okay, it's a funny name, but she's the only little girl hero I ever came across. See, she single-handedly rescues her sisters from an evil giant. The thing is, she can get away from him over the bridge of the single hair because she's light but he—"

"Is Molly Whuppie your role model?" asked Ned, trying

23

without success to keep the sneer out of his voice. "Because it's going to be tough to lose enough weight to get over that bridge yourself."

"Yeah, that's right, Ned. Thanks. What was I thinking?" I stood up. "Excuse me." Paul frowned. "The bathroom?"

"Down the hall."

I splashed my face with cold water and peered into the murky mirror. "Hello, dimwit," I said to my reflection. "Maybe tomorrow you should bring a stuffed teddy bear, huh? I bet that cute guy was impressed."

When I got back, the cute guy with the incredible blue eyes was speaking. "So I have the bad luck to be good at something that doesn't interest me very much and to be very interested in things—such as this—that don't pay the rent. That's about it." He shrugged.

"Thanks, Chris." Paul cast a scathing look in my direction and then turned a radiant smile on the final speaker. "Sheila. Please go ahead."

The woman sitting next to Chris, the woman he came in with and who was probably his girlfriend, introduced herself. Sheila wasn't beautiful but she was one of those women who got away with not being beautiful. She was beautifully put together in all the ways I was not.

"So why am I here?" Sheila smiled but her eyes didn't smile with her. "My real father took off before I was born. My mother married Harold when I was still a baby. Harold was a Negro. *And* he was my *real* real father." She fidgeted with her watch. "When I was ten, my mother planned a trip to see her sister in Alabama." She tucked her hair behind her ears. "My dad said he couldn't go but I told my mother I wasn't going if he didn't." She hesitated. This was hard, I could see. "When he explained why he couldn't, I called him a liar. I screamed at him." She looked down and tears spilled onto the table. She raised her face to us and I realized I'd been wrong. She *was* beautiful. "My dad died last year. He would've been proud, I think. I know I owe it to him to—to join this movement."

Paul, who'd been standing in the glare at the window, moved to the head of the table. "Thanks to each of you for your stories. I think that's enough for one session. Tomorrow night we'll talk about the philosophy of non-violence and we'll run through some techniques for protecting yourselves. See you all back here tomorrow evening."

We got up and filed out of the room. On the church steps I felt a hand on my arm. I turned around and my heart rate sped up.

"I liked your story." Chris looked sincere. I was still stinging from Ned's remark. "Molly Whuppie. It was cool. I never heard of it before."

I tried to think of something witty to say, something that might stay with Chris all the way home. Instead I blurted like a little kid, "I think Paul hates me."

A crooked smile dimpled his cheek. "Don't sweat it. Paul's one of those guys who takes himself way too seriously."

I nodded. It was an opinion I shared. I glanced around. "So where's Sheila?"

"I think she caught the bus. Why?"

"Oh. Nothing. I was just wondering." He looked like he was starting to lose interest in talking to me. "That was quite a story she told. It got to me."

"Yeah, me too."

"I'm sorry I missed your speech. What was all that stuff about being good at something you don't like?"

"I'm a civil engineer." He patted his shirt pocket. It was empty. "I wanted to be a poet laureate or a great concert pianist, but it turns out you need talent."

"I know what you mean. I was thinking of going into

archaeology myself, but they told me I had to have some sort of training. Looking for a cigarette?"

"Yeah, why? You have one?"

"Sorry. Don't smoke." We started down the steps. "So tell me—if I don't sound too much like Paul—why did *you* volunteer?"

"I'm not sure. Ah. Here they are." He took a pack of Camels from his jacket pocket. "Probably my high-minded upbringing. My dad's a Unitarian minister."

"Well, that trumps my Communist grandmother." He gave me a funny look. "I mean, they're ethical people, those Unitarians, but they don't have any dogma, do they?"

"I guess you don't know any Unitarians. Well, I'll see you tomorrow." He started away and then turned around. "Hey, don't worry about Paul. After this week, we'll probably never see him again."

4

THE NIGHT BEFORE we were to fly to New Orleans, it was stifling in my room and I couldn't sleep. I tried to cool my forehead against the glass of the partially open window. I'd never been able to force that window all the way up. There wasn't much air coming through it anyway since it faced the apartment building next-door, close enough for me to have borrowed their Colgate off the bathroom sill. T.J. had offered me the electric fan before she went to bed, but the blades were so bent, the damned thing clanked. I couldn't have slept with it in the room. Having grown up four to a bed, T.J. had more tolerance for noise than I did. Anyway, I wanted her to use the fan. I worried about her heart in this heat. In January a doctor had told her she needed tests to check out a murmur, but whenever I nagged her to make the appointment, she told me to *butt out*.

Apart from the muffled hammering of the fan blades in the next room and the usual barking dog, the night was almost quiet. Now and then the whoops and giggles of drinkers staggering out of Duffy's Tavern on the corner distracted me from the yapping mutt. Sometimes Duffy's customers paused to relieve themselves in the alley at one end of our apartment building's airspace. Until two in the morning, periodic streams of urine rattled against the tin door of the garage where Duffy stored his prize 1946 Hudson convertible. Rosemary said it was fitting that Duffy's beer should water that garage.

Tonight, for once, the tramps who slept in the alley were mute. One Sunday night in the early spring the skirmish below had cut out like a radio with its cord yanked. Someone shrieked, a sound that ended in a cough and then nothing. Before the scream died, I heard the slap of running feet, dwindling as somebody fled the alley. Then silence. When T.J. came in, I was zipping my jeans.

"I called the cops."

"I can't wait up here, T.J. It sounded bad."

"Hold on, I'll go down with you." She went back into her own room.

"There isn't time," I yelled, heading for the door. "You're not dressed—"

"I said I'll go with you." She came out pulling her coat on and jamming her feet into flip-flops.

I couldn't stop myself. "The doctor said you should throw those thongs away."

"Yeah, yeah, yeah," she snapped, trundling out the door.

"With your legs," I complained as we loped down the three flights of stairs.

"Yeah, yeah, yeah."

In the alley, the stench of urine almost pushed me back to the street. T.J. cut in front of me, shining a flashlight she'd had the foresight to bring. We spotted him crumpled against our building. His breath whistled like wind in a tunnel. It sounded leaky. He clutched his left side with both hands. I saw he wasn't a lot older than me. His dark skin was darker from weeks or months of not bathing, and he reeked. He lifted his eyes but I don't think he saw us.

"He stabbed me," he said, full of wonder.

T.J. bent and wrapped a torn length of sheet around his oozing ribs.

"I didn't do nothing," he said, pronouncing it "dint."

"Don't talk," T.J. told him.

"But I didn't do nothing."

T.J. turned to me. "Go out to the street. The cops won't know to turn in here."

The police arrived twenty-five minutes later. They hadn't brought an ambulance. It didn't matter. The drunk was dead.

* * *

Around four-thirty I finally slid into an uneasy sleep. Somebody's hound whined and scratched at my bedroom door. When I staggered over to open it, there was no dog, only T.J. with her blouse ripped open. Where one breast should have been was a pulsing tin pie plate. I put out my hand to make it be still. She stepped back from me. Then I noticed she clutched a small sleeping child to her other breast. As I drew close, she opened the blanket that had covered him, head to toe, and I saw he had no face.

"Jeri! Jeri! Wake up!"

I looked up at my grandmother and blinked. "What's going on?"

"You were yelling in your sleep."

I rubbed my eyes. "What time is it?"

"Time to get up."

5

I HAD DIFFICULTY navigating the steps down to the tarmac with my knees jiggling, but somehow I managed the descent without pitching onto my face. From the ground, the plane looked large but, from my point of view, not large enough. I wanted it to be gargantuan, invincible—roughly the size of the universe. The window of the cockpit looked ajar, which caused me to lurch up the portable steps and into the cabin before the pilot could pop his all-too-human head out the window. I wanted to sit with Thomasine, but when I stopped next to her, she said she needed to catch up on her sleep so I folded myself into a seat on the aisle next to Dorothy.

"You all right?"

I nodded cautiously. Keeping my seasick eyes open and fixed on the clean white cloth covering the forward headrest, I waited for the ocean tides to subside.

"Scared?" Very slowly I rolled my head toward Dorothy. "First time, huh?"

I nodded.

"You'll be okay. It takes some getting used to. We'll be rocking going up, just so you know."

"Goody."

She smiled and the cool receptionist in her face thawed away. "You can grab my arm if you need to. Just don't upchuck, okay? I can't take that."

"I can't promise."

"I really need you to do your best."

Chris sat with Sheila, across the aisle and one row ahead. I could make out their heads, blond leaning into brunette. Periodically, Sheila's silvery laughter or Chris's deep rumbling chuckles played cowboys and Indians in my stomach.

Across from me, Ned took some pains to precisely center a book by Nietzsche on his lap. His fingers looked raw. I turned over my copy of *To Kill a Mockingbird* so the cover wouldn't show. I didn't want Chris to see it. I wished I'd brought along something as profound as Nietzsche. Sheila, I was sure, would never read a cheesy bestseller like *Mockingbird*—I was just halfway through it and I could tell already it was a kids' book. Sheila and Chris were probably having a deep conversation about something really interesting. That's why he was sitting with her and I was over here with Dorothy.

The plane bounced into motion. I dug my fingers into the armrests and Dorothy patted my hand. When our speed increased, my heart jack-hammered. I swallowed and swallowed again. As we wobbled into the air, Dorothy tightened her hand around mine. I wanted to say thank you but I couldn't speak.

"We're okay," she kept saying. "We're fine."

I didn't feel fine. I wanted to pass out. I wanted to throw up. I wanted to stand up or lie down—anything but stay in that seat, waiting to plunge back to the ground. The wings rolled.

"Look at the stewardesses." They had unbuckled after

takeoff. "If you think something's wrong, Jeri, look at the stewardesses. They know what's going on."

But what if they don't, I thought. *What if they're as ignorant as the rest of us?*

"Would you care for something?" A pretty woman in a baby blue uniform and an army-style cap flashed me a confident smile and held out a tray of snacks. Her smile said, *This plane will not fall to the ground. Have some peanuts.*

I carefully shook my head. Anything that went in my mouth was going to make a U-turn.

Maybe over dinner in New Orleans I could say something to Chris about my book, something to show it wasn't what I normally read. I could say I picked it up in the airport lounge. Somebody could've left it there.

"Don't breathe so fast," said Dorothy. "You'll hyperventilate."

* * *

I tried imagining I was sitting in a large comfortable room with doors leading out to a lovely garden. I pretended that, if I wanted to, I could get up and stroll outside into the sun. But I had decided to sit quietly. Calmly. My choice. I opened *To Kill a Mockingbird*.

"You reading that?"

I started to say, "No, I'm checking the acid content of the paper." T.J. often told me I needed a trip switch for my mouth. I bit down on the inclination to be snotty. I could see Dorothy was trying to distract me. "Have you read it?"

"No. I've heard of it. Is it any good?"

"Not very."

"I wish I had more time to read. David's correspondence takes a lot of my time. He's involved in so many projects."

"Oh?"

"He's on several committees. He goes to three or four meetings a week. He's already down there, you know. On the Farm." I must've looked blank. "Parchman. The prison farm? I wanted to go down with him but I had a singing engagement."

"I guess you don't have any children."

Something changed in her face. "David wants to wait." She wasn't telling the truth. I was sure of it. Her tongue explored her molars, stretching her wide mouth and long jaw.

We bumped hard and I grabbed the armrests. Dorothy rubbed my wrist. "It's okay," she said in a liquid voice. The plane jerked again. The stewardesses were passing out snacks.

The plane stuttered into an atmospheric pothole and I gasped. Dorothy massaged my wrist some more. We were bucking hard now and I rammed the soles of my shoes against the floor, swallowing spit.

Another roll and I howled. Everyone except Thomasine turned to gape at me.

I placed my hands over my mouth. Dorothy grabbed a bag from the pocket in front of her and thrust it toward me. Then she slid toward the window. I opened the bag and heaved.

"I'm sorry," she said, standing. "I can't." She bent over Thomasine and shook her awake. "I've got to sit with you." Thomasine groaned.

I hunched over the bag, trembling, waiting for the next wave of nausea. It came, followed by a third wave. The only good news was I hadn't eaten breakfast.

"You want the window or you want to keep the aisle?" Chris stood next to me. When I didn't answer, he said, "Why don't you take the window? At least you can look at fresh air. Think you can manage to shove over?"

Somehow I made it into Dorothy's abandoned seat

without bringing on a fourth attack. "You all right? I mean, considering." I nodded, one hand around the bag, the other trying to paste wet strands back off my face.

"I'll take that," said the stewardess, leaning across him. "Here's another. Just in case. But you don't have to use it." I thought she was probably making a joke.

I gulped several times.

"It's all right," said Chris. "I'm cool. Go ahead and hurl."

* * *

I don't know how I managed to sleep, but I did. When I woke, Chris was reading *To Kill a Mockingbird*. He said, "Sorry. I didn't think you'd be looking at it any time soon."

"That's all right. It's boring anyway."

"You think so?"

"Don't you?"

"I like it."

"Well, I mean, I can see where it's going, can't you? Everybody all warm and cozy. Black and white together."

"Hardly."

"Well, I mean, Atticus and the cook—what's her name?— and the black church and all. And don't you just know noble Atticus is going to save the day for that man accused of raping a white woman? It's all so—so predictable."

"I think it's got some good things to say. Like, 'You never really understand a person until you consider things from his point of view.'" He closed the book. "How're you feeling?"

"I think I'm okay. Except for wanting to die."

"You think you might throw up some more?"

"God, I hope not. I'm so embarrassed."

"Forget it. Want your book?" I shook my head and he opened it again.

"You don't have to stay with me, Chris. I mean, I know your stuff's in the other seat. I'll be all right."

"No, you won't," he said without looking up. "You probably are going to throw up again. And when we start landing, you're definitely going to throw up again."

6

WILLIAM BLANCHARD was tall, with mocha-brown skin and reddish hair. Thomasine and Dorothy moved up to walk next to him. We must've made an odd sight, four white people parading through the New Orleans airport behind our dark-skinned leaders.

Blanchard led us to a dented Volkswagen bus. It was hot and cramped in there, but I felt so relieved to be on terra firma, I didn't care. Chris maneuvered me into the seat by the window. I pressed my face into the narrow opening and tried to pretend loud noises weren't coming out of my gurgling stomach.

When we pulled up to the parking booth, Blanchard held out his ticket and some cash. The attendant ignored it. Instead he bent down to peer into the van, staring at each of us for several seconds through dark sunglasses.

"These your relatives?" he asked. I didn't know whether he thought the question was funny or whether he meant it as a threat.

"Nassuh."

"Well, boy, in that case, who are they?"

"These two here be my cousins, suh." His accent was notably thicker than it had been when he greeted us. "But the folks back there, suh, they peoples done asked me could I give them a ride. I'm going right near where they want to get off so I said I thought it would be okay."

"Sure you ain't charging them, boy? You ain't licensed to be no taxi cab."

"Nassuh, but it might be they could help me out with gas."

"You need five white folks to help you pay for gas? Where you driving to, boy? Alaska?"

"Nassuh. My cousins gots to go over to Baton Rouge tomorrow because they grandma up that way in the hospital. And I has to drive them. So I needs to make myself some dollars . . ."

The parking attendant directed his sunglasses toward us once again. "If y'all came down for Mardi Gras, you either six months early or six months late."

Chris said, "I came down on business."

"So why not take a reg'lar taxi?"

Chris shrugged. "My boss doesn't like unnecessary expenditures."

The attendant adjusted his hat and fixed his gaze on Sheila. Behind us, the line of cars waiting to pay swelled. "Where you from?"

"San Francisco."

"And what'cha doing in Nawlins?"

"Visiting my sister."

"Oh yeah? Where she at?"

"She lives off Canal Street."

"What's her *ad*dress?" A horn bleated. The attendant

turned his head toward the sound but made no comment. He seemed to be chewing the inside of his cheek.

"Maybe you want to call up and get his exact address from the Louisiana highway patrol. That's who he works for."

The attendant tugged at his cap again. Then he waved us through.

* * *

I looked out at collapsing barns, lean-tos, and hovels. I saw a rusting plow abandoned in the field, as if someone had been too hot to take it back to the barn and then had forgotten it altogether. Garbage blew around empty pastures where skinny cows nudged the ground hopelessly. We passed a barefoot brown child of perhaps seven or eight, lugging a leaden sack of groceries. She kept her feet cool by walking in the weedy grass on the right-of-way, hopping as if something had stung a foot.

Sitting next to me, Thomasine fanned herself with June's *Modern Screen*. On the cover, Elizabeth Taylor's startling black eyebrows peeped out from a lethal hook of lacquered hair. On the other side of Thomasine, Dorothy mopped at her forehead with a lacy handkerchief.

Blanchard pulled into a gas station. I peered out the window and something shifted inside me with the violence of a small earthquake. There were the signs we came to tear down:

WHITE LADIES

WHITE MEN

COLORED

The **COLORED** sign hung askew on a rotting outhouse.

In the heat, the word seemed to quiver, as if it had been molded from pulsing black neon. Blanchard slammed the van door. Once outside, he lifted his hand in salute toward the small building that housed the station's general store.

"How do, Mister Jimmy."

Through the screen door, I could make out a stooped figure. He called out, "You go ahead and pump you some gas, Willie Bee. 'S too hot out there for me."

"Yassuh."

I turned toward Chris. "Willie Bee?"

"Cute, huh?"

* * *

William Blanchard drove us into a part of New Orleans I suspected few white tourists had ever seen. Porches hung from what looked to be a single nail. Here and there a wooden shutter tilted away from the house, tipping toward the street in a cockeyed salute. Most yards were bare dirt. I spotted a few old men and women sitting on listing porches, witnessing all that wasn't happening in the street.

We passed a playground swarming with children under the blind eyes of boarded windows. "Why'd they close that school?"

William glanced back at me. "That school ain't closed." He parked the VW. "Y'all be staying here with Miz Robinson." He waved his hand at Sheila and me. We clambered out. "Miz Robinson's little girl, Cassie, show you where you supposed to come for dinner."

I looked at the house. It was small but pretty, with a picket fence and a rose garden. The front porch looked solid.

Mrs. Robinson came out, wearing a pink uniform. "I has to go to work in a few minutes. But Cassie take good care of y'all."

Cassie looked about nine. She had ten pigtails and she was missing a canine tooth, making her grin infectious as she told us, "C'mon inside, y'all," beckoning with the pompous charm of tiny beings unaware of how tiny they are.

Mrs. Robinson had placed white lace doilies on the headrests of all the furniture. "Did you crochet these? They're pretty."

She tried to stifle her pride. "It ain't nothing. I would be teaching Cassie but she ain't got the patience. Step right in here, y'all. This here's where you sleep." We squeezed into a yellow-walled bedroom, the small bed under a lacework spread. Sheila admired the spread: "That's lovely, Mrs. Robinson. I've never seen one so intricate."

"You see, Cassie? Peoples appreciate the handwork."

"I likes to be outside," the child grumbled. "Don't want'a be in here making no old coverlet for no hope chest. I ain't hoping for nothing."

"You have a hope chest, Cassie?"

She shook her head. "Naw, but Mama say she gonna get me one once't I makes a quilt." She giggled. "So I expect I ain't never gonna have no hope chest."

Mrs. Robinson said, "Y'all gonna have to excuse me. I'm late getting to the hospital."

"I hope we didn't hold you up," said Sheila.

"Naw, nothing like that. I could'a gone on over but I wanted to be here when y'all came. So, Cassie, you remember the things we talked about."

"Yes, ma'am." As soon as her mother closed the front door, Cassie jumped up and started bouncing on the small bed. "You likes it here?"

"Very much."

"Yeah? What it be like in California?"

"California's okay too," Sheila said.

40

"Do colored go to school with white out there?" Sheila and I nodded. "They gots the same bathroom and everything?"

"They do."

A tall boy of about sixteen appeared at the bedroom door. "Y'all going on that Freedom Ride tomorrow?"

Cassie said, "This here be James, my brother."

"Naw, I'm not."

"Yes you is."

"Naw."

Cassie pushed him and he play-wrestled her off the bed and down on the floor. "Say uncle!" She shook her head, giggling.

"He always be saying he ain't my brother."

He let her up and dusted off his pants. "I shamed to be seen with you, gal."

"Well, I shamed of you!"

"A handsome boy like me? You crazy, girl?"

* * *

The Hardy Boys on my lap, I sat dozing on the front porch, dreaming about a black cook polishing my sneakers, and even in the dream I knew that had to be ridiculous. I thought I could hear Chris's voice saying you had to walk in someone else's shoes to really understand them. I realized he meant I was a bad person for letting the cook do work I needed to do for myself.

When I opened my eyes, he stood next to me, grinning. "If you think *To Kill a Mockingbird*'s predictable, wait'll you get deeper into *The Hardy Boys*."

I winced. "This was all I could find in the house. I must've left *Mockingbird* on the plane."

"Ned and I are headed over to Woolworth's for a sit-in. Want'a come along?"

I raced inside and splashed cold water on my face. My red cotton jeans looked like something out of the Montgomery Ward catalog, which they were, and my underarms had leaked big dark semicircles. The sight of Sheila asleep in her sleek black slip, one damp curl pasted to her cheek—*glowing*, not sweating like piggish me—should've put a stoplight on my crush on Chris. The rumpled girl in the mirror couldn't compete with her, that was obvious. Still, knowing things were stacked against me had never kept me from trying.

* * *

As we entered the five and dime, the odor of simmering lard and stale popcorn clobbered me. Lord, I was hungry. Even the vat of bubble-gum pink liquid bubbling on the counter looked delicious. A photograph of a tuna melt and French fries shimmered on the wall above the grill. My stomach groaned. Food was an eternity away.

We joined a group sitting at the counter with their hands folded, Thomasine and Dorothy with them. A few stools away, a woman in a sundress hovered over her blond son, a boy so pale and listless, I imagined T.J. calling him *peak-ed*, one of her favorite words. His mother was breaking crumbs from a cake-like slab of pollen-yellow cornbread but his head kept whipping away from her, as if he thought the cornbread might sting. I longed to reach over and snatch his plate.

A white woman a few stools away from us rose up with her water glass and flung it at us. The glass shattered, sending shards flying. Blood oozed from Dorothy's arm. She removed a sliver of glass and carefully placed it in an ashtray. The counter was awash, a small Niagara flowing onto the floor. A black man in a business suit came over with a mop and began cleaning up. "Ora Lee over there told me that's the store detective," Chris said. One of the waitresses, wearing big plastic earrings in the shape of a fork and a spoon, brought a rag.

"Sorry 'bout that," she said, sopping the water and picking up the ashtray with the glass shard. "You want something for your arm, hon?"

When the waitress went down the counter for a Band-Aid, a girl I didn't know whispered, "They used to throw coffee on us. Now they want'a know where we been whenever we be gone for a day."

"What do you mean, store detective?" I asked Chris. "He's black."

"I noticed that."

Someone behind me pulled my blouse out of my jeans. Stomach growling, I stared fixedly at the Coca Cola medallion, avoiding the photo of the grilled cheese sandwich. The blouse yanker socked my shoulder.

"Nigger lover."

She struck the side of my head, not forcefully enough to hurt, but somewhat gently, as if she thought she should test the waters and see how it went. I felt a ballooning desire to turn around and pop her in the face. The only thing giving her the courage to hit me was her certainty I would not hit back. What if I surprised her?

"You should be ashamed of yourself," the woman said. "You're an ugly stupid bitch and I wish you would die, nigger lover." She swung her purse at my head hard enough to knock me sideways. The waitress who had swabbed up the water rolled her eyes.

When my assailant swung her purse again, I slid from the stool to the floor and rolled into a ball, ignoring the water my pants were sucking up. Everything grew quiet. I thought I should pretend to fall asleep. That would get her. I kept repeating to myself, "I don't need to react, I don't need to react, I don't." After a while, someone tapped me on my back. "Jeri, it's me. Get up." Chris pulled me to my feet. "You okay?"

I looked around. "So, where did Ada the Hun go?"

"Some guy took her home. You're not hurt, are you?"

"Not a bit."

"It's time we got back for dinner."

"Oh, Chris! That's the nicest thing anyone's said to me today."

* * *

Sheila, having had a long nap, wasn't ready to go to bed after we ate. But there wasn't any place two white women could easily go in that neighborhood at night. We wound up sitting on the steps of the school. She pulled out a pack of cigarettes.

From the schoolyard we could hear the grunts and shouts of a group of boys playing basketball. The air was still and thick and wet.

Sheila smoked and I watched the kids moving over the court. One boy put his foot in a hole and twisted his ankle. He limped away with a buddy. It grew darker and one by one, they peeled off and disappeared.

Sparks flew from Sheila's cigarette as she tapped it on the edge of a step. "I don't think I've ever seen you with a cigarette."

"I don't usually smoke."

"Nervous about tomorrow?"

She didn't say anything for a bit. Then she looked over at me. "We'll be all right. We just have to stay cool."

"That's probably easier for you than for me," I said. "I don't have a lot of cool in me."

"I sensed that," she smiled.

I looked up at the moon. "Chris seems nice."

"Hmmm."

"I guess you guys are pretty tight."

"Not exactly." She sounded amused.

"He likes you, I can tell."

"Chris broke up with someone just before we left L.A. I think he's feeling pretty raw. They were together a long time."

"So what made them break up?"

"The Freedom Rides. Apparently she objected." She smoothed her hair and a jewel of some sort flashed from one earlobe.

"Well, don't worry," I said. "I can see he really likes you. It's not just 'cause he's on the rebound or something."

She cocked her head at me. "I'm not worried."

"Well, you do like him too, don't you?"

She shook her head. "Sure, but not that way."

"Why not? What's wrong with him?"

She chuckled. "From your point of view, I gather, nothing."

"But from your point of view?"

She smoked thoughtfully. Finally, she shrugged. "I don't date men, Jeri."

"What do you mean?"

She stubbed out her cigarette. "I think you can figure it out. You're not that young, are you?"

As she gathered up her cigarettes and her purse, it hit me. "Oh my god," I said. "Oh. Oh, I see. Christ, I'm sorry. Jeez, I'm really sorry, Sheila."

She arched one eyebrow. "What're you sorry for?"

"No. I mean, I think I must've sounded like I thought there was something—you know—wrong with it. I mean because I kept not getting it. Like it was too weird—oh, listen—I'm making it worse, aren't I?"

"You are."

"It should've occurred to me as soon as you said you didn't date men, but I was surprised because—well—"

"Because I don't look like your idea of a dyke?"

I rubbed my arms, as if I were cold, but I was embarrassed. I didn't know what to say, and not knowing what to say usually makes me say the wrong thing. "Well, yeah, I guess. I mean, you're really—you know—very feminine."

"You'd be astonished, Jeri, if you knew how many of your *feminine* girlfriends in high school had a crush on you."

That made me uncomfortable. I said, "Does Chris know?"

She shook her head, not in response but as if she couldn't believe what a child I was. "Yeah. I told him on the plane." She got up. "We'd better get back before they lock us out."

7

SHEILA GOT UP to smoke on the porch at midnight and then again around four in the morning. I pretended to be asleep. My question about her and Chris kept jabbing me in the solar plexus, like remembering the time I walked home from junior high with a big blood splotch on the back of my skirt.

It felt weird to be in a narrow bed, sleeping next to a lesbian. I tried not to brush against her. It might seem like an invitation. After all, it was the same thing as being in bed with a guy. It didn't matter that she wasn't interested in me. What mattered was I knew what she was and now it could look as if I was the one interested in her.

I'd only had sex twice in my life. The first time I was fifteen and he was eighteen, my best friend's brother. I was spending the night. Her family had money so her parents put me in their spare bedroom so "Lillian can get her beauty sleep." I woke up to find her brother next to me. "Just to cuddle," he said. I knew I ought to send him away but I was curious. He kept stroking me until finally I let him do it. It wasn't much. After that he bugged me to do it again but I kept telling him I had my period. I thought it would be bad manners to tell him what we'd done hadn't meant very much to me. "You'd better see a doctor," he snapped the last time he asked me. "You've had your period for six weeks straight."

The second time was better. I was sixteen and I'd been going out with Jamie for eight months. I thought someday we might get married. We did it in his family's basement and it was sweet. But after that he never spoke to me again.

Now I just kept thinking Sheila didn't look like a dyke. But, as soon as that word came into my head, it throbbed like a stubbed toe.

COLORED

NIGGER

DYKE

Jesus, I thought. *Maybe Sheila should picket me.*

* * *

At the train depot Chris stopped for cigarettes while the rest of us kept moving toward the platform. Ned took advantage of Chris's temporary absence to position himself next to Sheila. When Chris boarded, he found Ned in the seat he'd probably hoped to occupy. Since I was right behind them, he plopped down next to me.

"Welcome to the first day of the rest of your life," he said.

"Uh uh. That sounds too much like *welcome to the end of your life*." I leaned back and we didn't talk for a few miles. I kept imagining his eyes on me, but whenever I checked, he was staring past me, out the window.

Finally, he did look at me. "All that moss hanging off those cypress trees—it's creepy, don't you think?"

"They look grim, all right."

"When they dragged the rivers for Emmett Till, did you know they found plenty of other bodies?" I shook my head. "If they dragged that swamp over there right now, I wouldn't want to see what came out of it." His hands rested on his thighs. His fingernails were square and clean. I considered how terrific it would feel if he put one of those hands on top of mine.

Across the aisle Thomasine read her *Modern Screen*. I started to say something to him about how asinine Hollywood fan magazines were, but I realized Chris might think I was sneering at Thomasine, so I shut my mouth. I heard T.J. say, *Well, there's a first.*

"Do you live at home?" he asked me.

"At home?"

"That's a dumb question, isn't it? Where else would you live? I meant, do you live with your parents."

"No. My father's dead."

He studied my face as if it were an interesting diagram. "What about your mother?"

"Rita. Yes," I said, but I shook my head.

"You call your mother Rita?"

"She didn't raise me. My grandmother did."

"The Red."

"I live with her." We fell into an awkward pause and then, before I could stop myself, I blurted, "My mother's nuts."

"Excuse me?"

"Yeah, I mean it. She does crazy things. Like, she buys a hundred cases of fruit cocktail or she orders a side of beef when her freezer barely holds a tray of ice cubes. Of course, she can't afford any of it. T.J.—my grandma—has to run around after her, trying to keep her out of debtor's prison.

When my mother's not taking up hours of some travel agent's time, planning a gazillion-dollar trip, she's in the fetal position and God Himself couldn't get her up."

"That's rough."

I felt like my arms and legs didn't fit in their sockets, and my neck was out of kilter. "I'm used to it," I said, although that wasn't true. "My grandmother takes it a lot harder than I do." Why did talking about Rita feel like disloyalty? She *was* crazy, I didn't make it up. And Chris wasn't ever going to meet her, so what difference did it make if he knew? Plus, even if he did meet her, he'd figure out how batty she was in sixty seconds. I changed the subject. "You said your father's a minister?"

"I did."

"What about your mom? She take care of the rectory?"

"She died when I was twelve."

"Yeah? I was twelve when my dad went. But I wasn't living with him. He was back East somewhere, trying to get away from my mother. T.J. says Rita killed him, but I think she's at least half kidding."

"Sounds like I've got something in common with your grandmother. I half-think my dad killed my mother." I must've looked shocked because he added quickly, "Not in the flesh, of course."

"But how then?"

"You first. How did your mother kill your father?"

"Well, it's not my theory, it's T.J.'s. But I can see why she feels that way. Rita doesn't mean any harm but once she gets her hooks into you, watch out. She never lets go. She doesn't even know you want her to let go. T.J. told her a million times that my father divorced her but she never really believed it. He was her husband until he died. In her head, for all I know, he might still be her husband."

"Does your mother have hooks in you?"

I snorted. "She hardly knows I exist. I gave up on Rita a long time ago, on the theory you should always drop them before they drop you." I glanced over at him, remembering what Sheila had told me about his girlfriend dumping him. "Sorry. You know, too many times, my mouth gets going before my brain turns on. T.J. says I need a trip switch. I mean, all that stuff I said about my mother? I probably sound pretty cold to you."

"You don't sound cold, Jeri. You sound hurt."

I bit my lip. "So, your turn," I said. "What's wrong with your dad?"

He shrugged. "He's one of those impossibly good people who makes everyone else feel like shit. Stronger women than my mother might've done themselves in. Bless her, she had warm blood in her veins. She'd get riled and he'd sit there and look at her through those lizard eyes of his." He fumbled with his cigarettes. "Is this okay?"

"The cigarette? Sure."

"Is that true?" he asked me, putting a match in the ashtray. "Do you drop people before they drop you?"

"I wish. Listen, I've been dropped so many times, if a phrenologist checked my head, he'd get tired of reading bumps."

He stared at me, taking me in with those starry blue eyes. Then he laughed. "You've got the mouth."

"That's what T.J. says."

"What kid your age uses words like *phrenologist*?"

"Hey, don't call me a kid. You want to know where I got that word? Rita took me to see a phrenologist when I was twelve."

"Wild. So what was the prognosis?"

"That I would grow up to be a criminal. And here I am,

headed into a life of crime."

* * *

We pulled into the depot in Jackson at noon. I imagined the Klan crouched behind their pickups in the parking lot, waiting for us with baseball bats and tire irons, and my knees softened.

The other passengers fled even before we stood up. I heard Thomasine breathe, "Please, Lord, don't let these folks be nasty."

I said, "Amen to that."

At the bottom of the stairs, the depot looked small and shabby. I remembered T.J. saying waiting rooms didn't matter. She could've been right. How important was it, really, to take those signs down?

A porter, his dark face deeply notched, struggled with baggage as big as he was. His body was a sack of sharp bones. I smiled at him but he didn't smile back. He acted as if we weren't there. Yet as we began moving toward the depot, he knelt and fumbled with his shoelaces. Under cover of his hunched shoulders, his gnarled fingers flashed a crippled "V." I had to look away to keep from crying.

Except for the low hum of "Freedom Riders," "Freedom Riders," the depot was quiet. Sweat poured over my face and down my neck. I looked longingly at the water fountain, but it was guarded by a **WHITES ONLY** sign. I kept walking, but I had to pause for a toddler who burst through an open door, racing for the fountain. Just as the child's chubby hands stretched up toward the bowl, his rangy brown father grabbed him. As the little boy was carted back into the **COLORED WAITING ROOM**, a man in a flowered Hawaiian print shirt lunged at us, roaring like a demented lion.

"Fucking commies," he growled, swatting at Ned. I was

astounded to hear myself giggle. Dorothy frowned at me. Ned dropped to the ground, coiling into a snug ball as he'd been taught, his hands clamped across the back of his neck to deflect the kick. But no kick came. The rest of us stood around uncertainly.

The floral-shirted man weaved above Ned. Burrowed in slots of fat, the man's eyes oozed tears, or perhaps sweat, as he rubbed his wet face and wailed, "Fucking commie coon black sons a bitches . . ." Ned remained in that vaguely religious posture, looking as if he'd faced East too long and had toppled over. Finally, a Red Cap placed a dark protective arm around the fat man, leading him away with reassuring utterances. I kept looking over at the V-flashing porter, but his face showed nothing. He continued unloading luggage from the cart. As the Red Cap came back out, passing us without a glance, Ned struggled to his feet. His eyes slid toward me, probably to see whether I was sneering at him. Mirroring the porter, I raised my fingers in a V.

When we reached the **WHITES ONLY** waiting room, we walked unsteadily through the door and sat down. Captain Dawson and his men lined the wall, arms crossed, faces sealed up in boredom. This was our revolution, all movements telegraphed to the enemy in advance.

"This here's the waiting room just for whites," Captain Dawson announced. "Y'all gonna have to move on," he nudged Thomasine and Dorothy, "or I'm putting the lot of you under arrest." Captain Dawson repeated this speech and then repeated it again, and I thought of all the fairy tales in which the spell has to be cast three times. When the Captain went to court, he would tell the judge he was positive the culprits had heard him because he had thrice uttered the magical incantation.

I got up. I wasn't afraid anymore. I hated to think of T.J.

watching this sorry show, but I was mostly glad for it.

The starched, dun-colored shirts of the Jackson police stretched smoothly across their well-fed chests. They wore hats like those of army officers. One of them winked as he helped me up into the wagon. Brown curls sprang from under his cap and his green eyes reminded me of peeled grapes. I felt almost affectionate toward him and his fellow policemen. Maybe they knew the law they were enforcing was wrong.

Then the door slammed. The van lurched and rammed us into each other. From the cab, behind the mesh screening, we could hear the good old boys up front laughing at us. We hung on and sang.

> *We shall not, we shall not be moved!*
> *Just like the tree that's standing by the water,*
> *We shall not be moved!*

We joined hands and bellowed, some of us—like me—tone deaf. It didn't matter. That's the strange thing about singing. A bunch of people who can't carry a tune in a bucket, as T.J. would say—singing together, they can sound like the Mormon Tabernacle Choir.

8

THIS WASN'T the first time I'd been in Mississippi. And it wasn't the first time Mississippi had terrified me.

Three days after he'd been taken by his killers, the body of the boy from Chicago was pulled out of the Tallahatchie River. Every radio station and newspaper carried the gruesome details of Emmett Till's lynching. In Los Angeles, there were only a couple of days of summer left before school reopened. I'd been babysitting for the people in the apartment downstairs but they'd gone away on a camping trip, so I was at last free to do whatever I wanted.

Every morning after my grandmother left for work, I traveled to Mississippi over a bowl of oatmeal, a cup of cold sugary coffee, and the *Los Angeles Times*. While my foot tapped the floor, sunbeams cooked one bare leg. Whenever I catch a whiff of it, the baking-bread scent of sun on flesh brings back the horror of Emmett Till's last hours.

I don't remember seeing T.J. read the papers during that time and I don't remember her ever saying a word about

Emmett Till. But she couldn't have missed the story, and his ordeal must've made her remember what she wanted to forget.

T.J. grew up in Ricoh, an Indiana farming town. She had nine older brothers and sisters. By the time I came along, most of them were already dead from poor nutrition, alcohol, hard work, and smoking.

When she was ten years old, the family's barley farm disappeared in the 1920 Palm Sunday tornado. Her father went without work for the rest of his life. T.J. didn't know how long it had taken him to figure out he could only support his children by abandoning them. After that, her mother subsisted on handouts from the Catholic church, always far less than enough to feed growing children, especially a brood of that size. But they had some luck because an occasional under-the-table extra came from one neighbor or another and kept them from absolute starvation.

Every Tuesday the church sent out a large bosomy nun. She swept through the house that was little more than a shack, checking under beds and in the icebox and cupboards. A slice of cheese or a bit of meat set off an interrogation. Once she spotted a man's jacket in the closet and cut the family off for three months. The jacket belonged to T.J.'s oldest brother who had come from St. Louis for a visit. A visit from a male meant either he was eating the Church's charity or he was supplementing it.

T.J. said her mother kept shrinking, day by day, until light seemed to pass through her fingers as she scooped watery dollops of rice milk into the children's bowls. My great grandfather showed up now and then, looking for a little comfort, but he had to be ready to light out the back door whenever footsteps hit the front porch. The nun, a dedicated church servant, didn't mind conducting night raids.

Black families were few and far between in Indiana in those years, T.J. said, but Ricoh had one. They lived not far from her clan and, because that family had a bit more to eat and fewer children, the mother, a devout Christian named Ella—T.J. said none of the whites ever knew Ella's last name—saw it as her duty to share with those who were more needy. But she understood hand-outs from a dark hand would be hard for T.J.'s mother to accept, especially since, being one-quarter Iroquois, Mrs. Boyle didn't get a lot of respect herself. Ella had her eleven-year-old son leave a sack of meal or some apples or onions on their porch, late at night, very quietly. One night Nathan was caught on that porch by a group of white teenagers who accused him of stealing.

They were kicking him in the head when T.J. ran outside and screamed, "He was leaving it for us! He wasn't taking it!" The hoodlums kept kicking. "Look in our house. We don't have nothing, just look! They give us food." Her mother tried to pull T.J. inside. "Tell them," T.J. shouted at her. "Tell them he wasn't stealing, Mama!"

Her mother looked out at the road. There was a full moon and the boy's blood looked like pooled oil in the dirt. T.J. said she couldn't tell whether Nathan was out cold or too scared to make a sound. She wished he would say something. If he just said, "Please, Mrs. Boyle," wouldn't her mother have to defend him? Wouldn't she try to save him?

"Well, Mrs. Boyle, was he stealing from you or not?"

"How come you're not calling her Pocahontas like you always do?" T.J. screamed at them. "How come she's Mrs. Boyle all of a sudden?"

T.J.'s mother placed a hand on her daughter's shoulder and pulled her into the house. As she closed and bolted the door and T.J. fell to her knees, wailing, my grandmother said even then she wondered whether it wasn't the sweet sound of

"Mrs. Boyle" that had kept her mother pitilessly silent.

The boy was left in the road, his jaw hanging brokenly, his arms and legs shattered. No one moved him until his mother came. T.J. said seeing that woman was almost harder than listening to his screams. Her mother stayed in the house but the little girl who would become my grandmother went outside, went down to the road where the body lay. She wanted to tell Nathan's mother that she couldn't save him. But that would have meant breaking faith with her own mother. The woman never looked at her, didn't weep, didn't show any emotion. She only kneeled down in the dirt and cupped one hand around her child's torn face. T.J. stood above her, alone, sobbing. Nathan's mother lifted her son in her strong arms as if he were a sleeping infant and, without a glance at those who had betrayed him, carried him home.

* * *

At the Jackson police station we were shoved onto a bench and told to wait. Chris whispered to me that the two men in business suits were FBI. "Look at their shoes."

"What about them?"

"Shiny black oxfords."

A man in uniform gestured to me and I got up. He stood me in front of a white wall, looped a chain like a bib around my neck, and snapped my photograph. He snapped the first shot full-face and then ordered me to show the camera my right profile.

"Is that in case I escape and keep my head turned sideways for the rest of my life?"

He grabbed my hand and pressed my fingers onto an ink roller. I'd seen this done on television on *Dragnet*, but the people it was done to were criminals. When all my fingertips had been printed, he handed me a tiny wet paper towel.

Another cop, in dark pants and a white shirt with a badge on the pocket, ushered me over to the corner and told me to get on the scales. Three more men came over. One of them, with a fat face like pie-dough gashed by a slivered mouth and squinty eyes, spoke first. "What'cha think?"

A cop with a sparse white crew cut and glass-blue eyes, abstractly beautiful but chillingly vacant, said, "One-twenty?"

"Hell, naw. I'd bet at least one-twenty-five."

"More'n that, I'd say."

"Place your bets, gentlemen." The white-shirted cop, his hand over the balance bar, smiled merrily. "I'm waiting."

My head was on fire. "What do you think you're doing?"

The scrawny cop in a suit said, "I bet one-thirty-five."

Blue eyes said, "Put me down for one-twenty."

"Somebody ought to put you down," I said, "like they do with dogs."

The scrawny man said, "Are you white or a nigger?"

"Am I a what?"

"A nigger."

"I can't understand you. You must be speaking some ignorant local dialect."

"Put her down as a nigger."

"Well, for Christ's sakes," said the cop with a comb-over when the bar fell into place. "One-forty? She don't look fat. How the hell tall is she anyways?"

"She's a big 'un. Five nine."

"Jeez, you could'a fooled me. Tell you what, though, she don't look half that tall neither."

The merry cop nodded. "It's her boobs," he said. "Them jugs kind'a squeezes her off."

The gaunt man in the suit, the one I'd christened "the

undertaker," took my arm and dragged me toward a small room. I thought about kicking him, but clenched my teeth and warned myself to settle down. Another man, rounder but in a matching suit and those black oxfords, joined us and shut the door. The undertaker pushed me into a chair and hitched his butt over the edge of the table, facing me. His eyelids sagged. His pudgy partner spoke. "What is your race?"

I looked up at the reptile. "Would you please move back?" He grinned. His teeth were spotted and gray.

The heavy man said, "Miss Turner. Pay attention. What is your race?"

"How can I think with this bozo's butt in my face?"

The undertaker grinned. "You gotta think about what race you are?"

The fat man ignored his partner. "Are you a member of the Communist Party of America or of any other organization dedicated to overthrowing the United States government?" He'd said "guvmint" and I snorted. His eyebrows shot up. Below them, his gray eyes were flinty.

"Who are you two?"

"We're the ones asking the questions."

"Are you the FBI? You are. You're the FBI." I sat back in my chair. "Bobby Kennedy sent you down here to ask me these—these—?" I couldn't think of the right word. "These *illegal* questions?"

To me, they were indistinguishable from one another, except that one was short, one tall, one lean, one fat. If I'd met them on the street an hour later, I wouldn't have recognized either of them.

"Let me get this. You're paid to sit around and make bets on a person's weight—?"

He leaned back toward me. "Stop playing games, girly. Are you white or nigruh?"

My nostrils drew together. His breath reeked. "That's not really something anybody knows for sure about themselves, is it?"

"I would take this more seriously if I were you, Miss Turner," said the fat agent. His expression seemed half-gentle, and, for an instant, I almost believed he wished me well. "Whatever you tell us goes into your permanent record in Washington, D.C. If you're not a Negro and not a Communist, I'd think you'd want to get those facts into the record."

"Put this in your record. That awful man bet on me like I was some sort of animal. I want you to write that down. Write it down! I want him brought up on charges." The skinny man snickered. "Write down that he's a horse's ass too."

The horse's ass snickered again. Then he reached out and flicked his fingertips at my nipple. It stung. Before I could stop myself, I had jumped up and was yanking on his skimpy hair. His fat partner spun me around and started slapping me mechanically, only on my left cheek, his rubber-skinned face smooth and colorless. I stumbled backward and a sharp pain tore through my scalp. The undertaker circled me, waving a little wad of my hair, and incredibly all that went through my mind was I'd been mistaken, they were very different from each other. The undertaker's face was radiant, his eyes bright. He brushed my hot cheek with wisps of my hair.

"There you go," he crooned. "There you go, little girl. Play with fire, gonna get burned, little girl."

"Now I am a Communist!" I screamed as his partner propelled me toward the door. "If horrible people like you hate them, I want to be one."

Dorothy stood on the scales. She frowned at me and I thought she looked like an irritated receptionist. Chris called out, "You okay, Jeri?"

"I'm a Communist!" I shouted to him, like someone

blowing kisses. "They made me a Communist!"

* * *

Two burly cops lifted me off my feet and hustled me across the street to the Hinds County Jail. There, after confiscating my shoes, a heavy-lidded matron put me in a tiny cell without saying a word. "Hey, wait," I called to her back. "Where's lunch? It's been a long time since breakfast!" The sole answer I got was the metallic banging of another door.

There was scarcely enough room to turn around. Something sticky coated the cement floor so I drew my bare feet up into one of the four bunks stacked against two walls. I was almost asleep when the matron brought in Thomasine and Dorothy. I said again, "Please? Couldn't we have some food?" and again she ignored me.

Thomasine gaped. "Hey, look at your face, girl—one side's beet red."

"Tell me about it." I combed my fingers through my hair. *Ouch.*

Dorothy, from the top bunk across from where I sat scowled at me. "Why did you tell everybody you were a Communist? You know what Paul said. That's not something to joke about."

"I wasn't joking. Didn't you hear those jerks making bets on my weight?"

"So what?"

"The scrawny guy zapped my breast. He's not allowed to put his hands on my breasts."

Dorothy heaved a long irritable sigh. "Where did you think you were coming? To a Scottish picnic?"

"I didn't think I'd be molested."

"You don't know what it is to be molested. Why did you pull that man's hair?"

Thomasine, who had started to lie down, shot back up. "You didn't!"

I felt sullen. "How'd you know?"

"Someone told the deputy while they were carrying you out. It's probably going to be in tomorrow's newspaper, but I expect that's what you were hoping." She lay down and turned her back to me.

"All I did was pull on it a little—I didn't yank it out—but they took out some of mine." I tipped my head so Thomasine could see.

"Girl, there's some blood."

Dorothy rolled back over to glare at me. "First you break your oath to be nonviolent and then you tell everybody we're Communists. You're a real prize, you know it?"

"I didn't say *we* were Communists, Dorothy. I said I was." I pulled my shirt away from my breasts and blew downward. "They shouldn't be asking that stuff. It's none of their business."

"The segregationists tell everybody the Communist Party's behind our movement, they claim we're just trying to start trouble so the Reds can take over the country. And a lot of Americans believe them. We need to prove it isn't true."

"The segregationists aren't going to say anything nice about us no matter what we do, so what difference does it make? If people believe in our cause, they won't listen."

She swung her legs off the bunk. For an instant, I thought she might jump down and slap me. But, of course, she'd sworn an oath to be non-violent, so she stayed where she was. "Don't forget who paid for you to come down here. CORE didn't do that so you could give us a black eye."

I put my hands on my hips. "This Movement's not only about taking down signs."

"I see. Now you're going to explain the Movement to

63

me? Based on your—what? One week of experience?"

"I don't need a lot of experience to know we're fighting for constitutional rights. And I know the Constitution says nobody has the right to ask me those questions."

"Doesn't it dawn on you that there are hundreds of thousands of citizens in this country who don't have any rights at all? None? Oh, forget it." She lay back down and closed her eyes. "There's no point in talking to a fool."

Thomasine folded up her movie magazine and thumped her leg with it. After a moment, she looked at me as if she'd just seen me. "What're you doing in here, Jeri? You should be over on the other side with Sheila."

"When they asked me if I was a Negro, I told them I didn't know for sure."

She smiled thinly. "Too bad they didn't ask me. I don't know for sure either."

* * *

We were taken down to the courtroom the next morning. The room was crowded with people and at first I couldn't figure out who was the judge. Everybody was talking at once, calling out numbers and names. There was no way to tell which guilty bang of the gavel was supposed to be mine, if I even got one all to myself. I did wonder if I'd be charged for attacking the federal agent, but I figured those guys wouldn't report what I'd done because then they'd have to say what they did. And I could testify against them.

If Paul Warren hadn't told us, I would've had no idea we'd been sentenced to six months of lockdown in maximum security at Parchman Farm. How many sharecroppers had stood in that courtroom, wondering what had just happened? It had to be mighty scary to be hauled off to prison when you had no idea how long you were going to be there.

None of us expected to do the six months. Paul had told us to stay in for forty days, after which the lawyer would plead *nolo contendere*. Then we'd be released. I wondered if the forty days were supposed to have Biblical significance.

Chris said, "You look swollen. Let me see." He reached for my sunglasses.

Mosquitoes had feasted on my eyes all night. When I got up that morning, Thomasine blurted, "Holy shit!"

I backed away from Chris's hand. "Never mind."

"Don't be so vain."

One of the guards was smoking. The odor from his burning tobacco made me think of the bums who slept in the alley below our apartment in Los Angeles. And I thought too about the young bum who died before anyone except T.J. came to save him.

Chris snatched off my sunglasses. "Christ. What did they do to you?"

I grabbed my glasses back and jammed them on my face. "I'm allergic to mosquitoes."

"Maybe you ought to have something—some kind of shot? You look pretty bad."

"So much for my vanity."

"You should ask to see a doctor."

"I wouldn't trust a Southern doctor to give me aspirin."

"They graduate from the same programs as the doctors in the North, Jeri."

"It's not their medical training, it's that they probably hate us."

The deputies were beginning to herd us toward the door. "Your cheek's a little bluish," Chris said. "They hit you?"

"Well, yeah, but I started it. I pulled the undertaker's hair."

"You did what? What undertaker?"

"That scrawny FBI guy."

"You pulled his hair?"

"I know, I know. Dorothy's really mad at me. But didn't you hear them making bets on what I weigh, Chris? And that guy—touched me."

"What do you mean, *touched you*?"

"You know." I put my hand on my breast. "Here. Then I lost it."

"Damn," he said. "You're a barrel of surprises, Geraldine Turner."

"Get a move on," said one of the deputies, rolling us out by our shoulders as if we were bowling balls.

I was the last to climb into the van. Dorothy, across from me, shot me an accusing look and shut her eyes. A wild bump nearly threw her toward my lap. Chris seemed to be dozing, but he managed to keep her from falling onto me.

This was far worse than the short ride through Jackson from the train station to the police station. On an empty country road, the paddy wagon veered and pitched from one side to the other as we rattled around like dishes falling off a shelf. Every so often, the driver violently slammed on the brakes. We tried singing, but it was hard work keeping our seats on the narrow benches. We could hear the two of them in the cab chortling whenever one of us yelped.

About an hour out of Jackson, the driver stopped by the side of the road. Through the grilled windows we could see we were in the middle of nowhere. Thomasine looked over at me. "What're they doing?"

"I know. We aren't there yet," I said, breathing hard. "I don't think we're even close."

The back doors opened. Two men stood in the opening, the glare of the sun behind them. Courthouse deputies had loaded us into the van so we hadn't seen these men before.

One was close to my age with yellow hair and skin so pale, he might have been albino, except his eyes were flat black. The other, somewhere in his forties, had a face of knobs, his disfigurement looking like the result of years in a boxing ring.

"How come they so butt ugly?"

The kid shook his head. "Beats me."

"They send us the sorriest gals they got. You'd think they could find us one or two good-looking ones. Maybe by accident. This begins to look like some kind of plot."

"That one over there ain't too homely," said the kid, pointing at Sheila.

"Too skinny. But take this one, now." He poked me. I recoiled into Thomasine. "She ain't half-bad. Take off those peepers and let's have a look-see."

I tried not to breathe, not to move, my heart thumping so hard, I thought my T-shirt might be moving up and down. Across from me, Dorothy gave a warning shake of her head. Chris's jaw was clenched.

"I said, take them off." He reached toward my face. Chris leaned forward but Dorothy put a hand on his arm.

"You like colored girls?" she said.

Knob-face turned to her. "What you talking about, gal?"

"She's got good hair and all but that girl's just as colored as me. You saw them bring us out together, didn't you? You like dark meat? That's okay, then, just be careful you don't catch something. I believe this gal's made the rounds, if you know what I mean."

"Shut your hole, nigger." He hesitated a moment but then slammed the van doors.

I wanted to kiss her but her yellow eyes looked through me and she didn't say another word until we reached the prison.

9

I DON'T KNOW what I expected, but not what we saw when we were taken out of the van. The building looked new, a boring concrete block with narrow barred windows under the roofline. The sky was dotted by puffy white clouds. I thought, *maybe this is a fairy tale.*

The guards took Chris and Ned down a separate corridor. After a few minutes, a huge white woman came out and shoved the four of us into an icy room. Given the oppressive heat outside, the air conditioning felt good at first, but pretty soon I started to shiver in my damp shirt.

After the white woman disappeared, I huddled with the others on a wooden bench until a black girl came out. She pointed at Sheila, who got up and followed her through the door. Thomasine said, "She must be a trusty."

"What's a trusty?"

"Prisoners who work and get privileges."

"Her work is pointing?"

"You are funny, girl."

After several minutes, the trusty came back out and nodded at Thomasine. "Here goes nothing," she whispered to me. The girl stood to one side of the door and Thomasine squeezed by her. After another long wait, Dorothy went in and I sat on that bench by myself, rubbing my arms. Waiting for whatever was going on in there. This part I hadn't known about. Were they simply handing out the skirts? *Sure*, I thought. *And doing a careful fitting*.

Finally, the dark-skinned girl came out and smiled knowingly at me, beckoning with her finger.

I started into the room, but she blocked me. "If you pleases," she said, holding out her smooth tan palm. I looked into it. Was she expecting a donation? "Miss Marilyn Monroe," she drawled. I understood then and removed my sunglasses. Her eyes widened. "Hooey," she breathed, "they sure done done a job on you."

The white woman behind the door, wisps of greasy hair sticking to her neck, stood with her back to me, wheezing asthmatically. The room was small and miserably hot—the air conditioning blasting the other room didn't reach this one. I took in a doctor's examining table and a single folding metal chair. The vinyl cover on the table was grimy. On the floor stood a bucket of murky water.

Barnyard odors wafted off the woman's massive body. Scarlet striated the sallow flesh of her legs, and her ankles, resembling cheap socks, rippled over the tops of her shoes. With every move, she chuffed like a dying engine.

Coming in behind me, the trusty murmured, "Take off your drawers."

That this grubby sweating woman wanted to put her hands inside me caused me to sway on my feet. A terrifying image swept my mind—some shadow of her dirty hands wedged inside me forever. I'd never be able to wash her off, never get the stench of her out of me. I told myself, *She doesn't have the right to do this*. But Dorothy sneered, *Do you know how many people have no rights? Did you think you were coming on a picnic?*

"Get up there," said the fat lady.

Sheila had submitted. Thomasine had submitted. Even Dorothy must have submitted. I hadn't heard any struggles. I hadn't heard screaming. I was the only one who would make a fuss. The matron's arms were larger than my thighs. There was clearly no use in making a fuss. I would lose and no one would sympathize with me when they brought me to the other Freedom Riders, black and blue, my face even more swollen than it already was.

I climbed up on the table and gritted my teeth.

With a grunt, she bent to dip her hand in the water. My breath came in quick sharp gasps as she dug into my thighs and then jabbed one finger into my rectum. A squawk burped out of me. Ignoring it, she removed her finger and plunged it into my vagina, her long fingernail raking my insides through the rubber glove.

The trusty stood and watched, perhaps to discover whether I was as tough as my puffy face suggested.

I sat up gingerly, blinking fast, my face turned to the wall. I kept reminding myself of T.J.'s words: A*n injured bird gets pecked to death*. That was practically the first thing she ever taught me. My voice cracking, but my chin lifted, I said, "Find anything interesting?"

The matron peeled off her rubber glove and tossed it into the water bucket, signaling the trusty to take me away.

* * *

I stood with my back pressed against the bars. The cell was a lot smaller than I'd expected. Dorothy sat on the bottom bunk. "You're not having another attack like on the plane?"

"I'm trying not to."

"Just breathe. Try to slow it down or you're going to upchuck again. Please do not upchuck. I cannot deal with throw-up."

We had two steel bunks, one on top of the other, and two thin mattresses. No pillow and only two light blankets. The air conditioning gusted through the cell. I saw a sink and toilet. On the cement floor there was just enough space for one of us to lie down alongside the bunks, if we ever wanted to lie down there with the bugs that were sure to come out when it got dark.

I climbed to the top bunk and put my head between my knees.

"Think of something you like."

"Like what?"

"Want the Bible? It's down here."

"That's it, huh? A Bible?"

"It would do you some good to read it."

I hesitated. It was the only reading material we were going to have. "Okay, give it to me." I opened to Genesis and tried to find a comfortable reading position. That was a lost cause. For half an hour, I browsed the pages without landing on anything I cared to stick with. Finally, I handed the book back down to Dorothy. "Sorry. I'd rather read a badly written mystery. Are you still mad at me?"

I heard her turn on her mattress. "Let's not talk about it."

"I want to talk about it."

"Well, you don't always get what you want, Jeri. Even when your skin's white."

"Is that what you're holding against me?"

"I'm holding against you that you lost your temper.

Because you could. And you could because you're white."

"You're wrong. They thought I was a Negro."

"Don't be ridiculous." Dorothy stood and put her hands on my bunk. "We've got to get along. So let's agree not to talk about this, okay?"

"I won't agree to that."

"I keep forgetting how young you are."

"Decent people aren't going to turn against the Movement because of me saying I was a Communist."

She went to the bars and looked into the corridor. "You know, I think some white people join the Movement because they're not happy being superior to Negroes. They have to have more. They have to be superior as well to people who think they're superior to Negroes."

* * *

We heard, "Man coming!" and the banging of the gate at the end of the cellblock as it slammed shut. Mrs. Buckerfield, the fat woman with the sharp fingernail, waddled in first. Behind her a man pushed a cart filled with trays of food.

"He's a Negro," I whispered to Dorothy.

"Yes, he is."

"But they're letting him in here with white women."

Dorothy looked down at the white bread and stewed apricots, up at the wall, down again, and then stood and pushed her tray back through the slot. She went to the sink and began washing her hands. I noticed there wasn't any soap.

I chewed on the fried lunchmeat. It tasted okay. I thought I might give the apricots a pass. "I didn't think they'd do that. Let a Negro man in here with white women."

She lay down on the floor and started doing sit-ups. "Male slaves used to stand around while the mistress got dressed. You don't put a dog out before you take off your clothes."

"Well, that doesn't make any sense. How come Emmett Till was lynched if they don't care?"

"Emmett Till acted like a human being," she said. "That was his mistake."

* * *

Freedom Riders filled up the cellblock. Dorothy said the authorities wanted to keep us away from the other prisoners so we wouldn't contaminate them with our radical ideas. Except that we couldn't see each other, it seemed like my idea of a college dormitory. The women laughed and called out all day. At night they sang a dirge. I thought that was pretty funny.

Now the day is over
Night is drawing nigh
Shadows of the evening
Steal . . . across . . . the sky

The lights never dimmed but I'd climb up into my bunk and, through a narrow bank of windows, I'd watch the sky turn pink and then inky. From up there I'd listen to the evening's entertainment. A few times Dorothy sang, once what she called an aria from Rigoletto. I'd never heard of a composer named Rigoletto, but her singing sounded great and I told her so. She granted me a smile, the first from her to me since we were at the Jackson police station.

Sometimes, late at night, when the cellblock finally grew quiet, I thought I heard a voice coming through the toilet vent, not calling out to us but just talking, maybe to himself. He sounded weirdly happy.

10

Dear Jeri,

████████████████████████████████████

talking a blue streak. I took the bus.

████████████████████████████████████

Here we go again.

████████████████████████████████████

When are you coming home?
Love, T.J.

WHEN T.J. SAID, "Here we go again," the tour guide was sure to be Rita gliding off planet earth in some way that might amuse anyone who had not made the journey with her. Seeing those words preceded by a black bar filled me with appreciation for Parchman's censor.

There was the time Rita brought home a fifteen-foot Christmas tree for an apartment with a nine-foot ceiling. She'd telephoned eleven times while T.J. was at work. "Be sure she comes over as soon as she gets home, Jeri. I want her to see this. It's magical." I thought T.J. would say she had to eat dinner first, she usually came home starved. But no, she took me and we walked the ten blocks to Rita's place. I've never seen my mother happier. Even at eight years old I knew better than to point out that the top six feet of the tree were crawling across the ceiling.

When I was twelve, Rita showed up while T.J. was at work, with a plan to immigrate to Canada and take me with her. "We can live with the Eskimos. They're groovy people, very spiritual, very deep.

"When I was in high school I took a pottery class and the instructor said my pots were worth a fortune. We could make our living up there. I'd do pottery all day. They probably have public kilns, you know? And it's really cheap to live on the reservation."

By the time I turned nine, I knew how to stall Rita whenever she was *trapped in an air pocket*, as T.J. put it. Under water, but breathing. I asked my mother to tell me the history of the Eskimos. I asked her what their art looked like. The only wrong move I made was to ask if she actually qualified to live on the reservation.

"Of course I qualify," she said. "My grandmother—your great-grandmother—was a full-blooded Iroquois." She was off by three quarters but there was never a point in presenting facts to my mother.

When T.J. came home, Rita was still babbling away. T.J. told me to put two frozen chicken potpies in the oven and wait while she walked my mother home.

If my grandmother or I had ever needed proof that Rita was an inescapable commitment—which we didn't—we got it from my father's failed shot at a clean getaway. He wanted to remarry. I'd met his fiancée. I had to assume living with a colorful woman had driven him to appreciate a colorless one.

Her name was Nan or Pam or something like that, and she was no match for my flamboyant mother. Rita showed up at the chapel, arms chockablock with flowers. When she deposited them on the floor near the altar, the minister noticed they were funeral wreaths.

Somehow she found the room where the bride was dressing and burst in to congratulate her. And congratulate her. And congratulate her. But then Rita's gaze fixed on the woman's hairdo. "Wrong!" she pronounced. "Alistair will hate it." Although my father's name was Carl, Rita always called him Alistair. I never knew why. She took a pair of scissors from her purse and approached the bride with every intention of "evening out" the layers of Nan's or Pam's hairdo, as she later explained with elaborate innocence when T.J. asked her what the hell she thought she was doing. My father's betrothed fled the chapel but not before screaming at him for fifteen minutes about the fruitcake he'd picked for a first wife.

I didn't want to know what Rita was up to now.

* * *

At the end of our cellblock, Mrs. Buckerfield was taking her nightly shower, bawling out the only song she seemed to know:

> *Yesterday my man done gone away*
> *I stayed in bed, all black and blue—*
> *Before he left, he had no word to say,*
> *I never got a single I love you*

When the pounding of water stopped, I thought I heard tapping on metal but it lasted only a second or two, so I wasn't sure. The block had grown dead quiet. I realized all of us were waiting for the gate to open and shut, for the matron to pad off on her wide feet. But the door didn't clang and her feet didn't make a sound. She had to be lurking there, spying on us as we listened to her listening.

"I hear y'all," she yelled finally. "What'cha up to?"

A black woman from Pittsburgh, whose name was Cora Lee, called out, "Nothing, Mrs. Buckerfield."

"Don't give me that. I hear y'all banging."

"We're only banging on the pipes because the water doesn't run fast enough in our sink."

"Leave them pipes alone, y'all hear me? I'll get Captain Ray in here if you don't. He's liable to take your mattresses."

A moment later the gate slammed. I hung over the edge and looked at Dorothy. "What do you think's going on?"

Her hands were folded on her stomach. "You know everything I know."

Earlier, Hannah, one cell over, had given me the block's only pencil along with the Bible to write against. On a long strand of toilet paper, I'd been trying to compose something to T.J., but I was distracted by my memory of a night when I was about fourteen or fifteen, sitting at the kitchen table working out rebuses printed on the insides of bottle caps. My grandmother and Irene, a friend of hers from her Communist Party days, were downing Lucky Lagers. Eight fat brown empties squatted between them. I'd stacked the caps and was making my way through the puzzles printed inside them. Irene was talking about a woman named Lydia, someone from the old days who, according to her, "loved humanity only in the abstract and never in the particular."

T.J. took a swig of Lucky and waggled the bottle. "Maybe loving humanity in the abstract's the way to go, Irene. Think about it. Looking too close at mankind in the singular can undermine a hell of a lot of good intentions."

I chewed on the pencil and squinted at the darkening sky through the narrow prison window. When I remembered what T.J. had said, I felt ashamed. It looked like I was one of those people who only cared about black people *in the abstract*. I sure didn't have a caring relationship with the one in my cell. True, Dorothy didn't like me any better than I liked her. But she wasn't a bad person. She'd been kind to me on the plane, at least until I vomited. And I admitted to myself that at least some of the things she'd said to me when she was angry were true. I had promised to be non-violent and I had broken that promise. And lately I'd begun to realize that it was petty to make a scene just because some creep flicked my nipple. Most black women had gone through far worse, so I couldn't entirely fault Dorothy for believing I was a spoiled white brat who assumed she was entitled to justice when nobody else could get it.

But my problem was she seemed so *un*-black—I didn't know black people could be uptight. It struck me that that was a prejudiced thought, but I couldn't stop myself from thinking it. The other Freedom Riders shouted, "Send down the bug killer!" and Dorothy would click her tongue, saying it was sacrilegious to mash insects with the Word of God.

Someone called out, "I've made contact with the men behind us."

I put down the pencil. "Was that Kitty?"

"Sounded like her."

I peered down again. "What men is she talking about?" Dorothy just shook her head.

"Is that what all that banging was about?" Hannah, next to us, sounded like white Southern vamp. "Some kind of signal, was it?"

Kitty said it was and Thomasine called out: "Are those guys in solitary?"

"Yeah, and the one I'm talking to has been telling me they're starving over there."

Hannah snickered. "Big surprise."

"But they don't have to starve. We could we give them some of our bread. We get enough."

Hannah was skeptical. "Should we ask the trusties to carry it over there, Kitty?"

"I'm serious. The guy—Tyrell—told me if I could get it through the vent, he thought he could reach it."

"So it was *his* idea."

"What difference does that make, Hannah?"

"What if a guard comes through when you're passing the bread?" said Thomasine.

"If y'all even can."

Cora Lee asked her, "What is it, Hannah? You don't want to give up your bread?"

"It sounds hare-brained to me, y'all. Y'all going to wind up getting those men in hot water."

Kitty ignored her. "Tyrell used to be a trusty. He's seen the corridor that runs behind our cells and he says the guards just about never go in there. It's a tight squeeze."

"It's fine with me to give them our bread," said Sheila. "But I don't see how you're going to do it. How wide is the corridor?"

"He doesn't really know but he says you couldn't lay down across it."

"That doesn't mean y'all can get a boatload of biscuits across it."

"All right, Hannah," said Cora Lee. "We know your position. So cool it, okay?"

"I think I can do this. Just wrap all the bread in a net off a Kotex and tie it up with string from my mattress. I've already pulled enough out."

"And then what? In case y'all haven't noticed, there are walls between us and them."

"Yes, Hannah, but those walls break at the vents. So if

I stick my arm up there and swing—I thought of using my toothbrush as a weight. Tyrell puts his arm up his side and grabs the toothbrush—voilà! We've got a pulley."

"All in favor?" said Cora Lee. "Or maybe we just count those opposed. Anybody besides Hannah?"

No one spoke.

* * *

That evening the trusty who had taken my sunglasses—Hannah said her name was Iola—collected our trays and the prison grew quiet. Kitty called out, "C'mon, ladies. Make some noise. Otherwise Duchess Buckerfield's going to get suspicious."

"I could tell a funny story," said Sheila.

Cora Lee approved. "You're on."

"It's about an interracial couple named Wilma and Al. Wilma's Negro."

A gate slammed somewhere. I felt alarm vibrate through the cellblock. After a moment, the prison receded again.

"Keep talking," said Kitty.

"Okay. Where was I? Oh yeah. Wilma had family in Louisiana. Al told my dad they were going out there to visit her folks. My dad said, 'Are you going to fly?' and Al said, 'Hell, no. Too damned expensive. We're driving.' My dad told him, 'You're crazy.'"

I thought of Harold, who couldn't make a trip South with his family. It must've been tough for him to hear a white man say he wasn't afraid to do it.

"So there they were, looking for a place to eat lunch in some small town in Arkansas. Al saw a restaurant and parked in the lot behind it. Wilma said she didn't think it was a good idea, she was sure the place only served white people. Al said, 'Well, I'm white, ain't I?'

"Wilma told my mother the restaurant was posh but empty. All the tables were covered in white linen. It looked so classy, she started shaking. She told him, 'Al, we've got these kids. We can't get ourselves thrown in jail.'"

Just then the gate clanged. Mrs. Buckerfield had come in. Kitty said sharply, "C'mon, Sheila, we're listening. What did Al say?"

"Yeah. Okay." Sheila's voice sounded quaky.

"They couldn't get arrested," Cora Lee prompted her. "Because of the kids."

"Yes, that's right. So Al said nobody was going to throw him in jail and as long as Wilma was with him, nobody was going to throw her in jail either. He would make damned sure of that. She's kind of timid so she followed him inside, the kids stringing along behind her. She thought her kids looked even more scared than she felt, although, being raised in San Francisco, they probably didn't know what they had to be scared of. Wilma's carrying the baby and they're standing around the reception desk. She tells my mom they must've looked pretty scruffy, they'd been on the road for a couple of days by then. She said she was hoping they'd just get thrown out and that would be the end of it.

"After a minute or so, a waitress comes out and takes a good long look at them. Then she turns around and goes away. A couple of minutes after that, out comes a man. He's got this mean face and he looks at them real hard. Wilma's practically peeing her pants. She knows he's going to go in the back and call the cops and she's going to lose her kids and she and Al are going to jail. But the man doesn't go in the back. He turns around and bends over the desk, grabbing some menus, and then he says to Al, 'Right this way, sir,' and he takes them all the way to the back of the empty restaurant. Some dark corner. But he holds the chair for Wilma and sends the waitress to get a high chair for the baby and a booster seat for their toddler. That waitress didn't look too happy, Wilma said, but she took their order and a Negro in a white uniform came out and filled up their water glasses."

The gate clanged again. Mrs. Buckerfield was gone. I felt a collective sigh of relief ripple through the cells.

"Al told us it was some of the best food he ever ate on the road. He was glad they stopped there, even though it was a bit pricey. They paid the bill and Al left a nice tip. They gathered up the kids and went out to the parking lot. Wilma gets in the front seat. But she sees the back door of the restaurant start to open. She told us her heart dropped into her stomach and she says, 'Oh, my lord, Al, we're in big trouble—'"

"I did it!" Kitty cried. "I did it! It worked!"

"That's terrific," said Cora Lee. "Good work, Kitty. Tomorrow we'll start sending our bread over. Now, Sheila, finish your story. We want to hear what happened."

"Yeah, right. Anyway, Wilma sees that the people coming out are all Negroes. Six of them. They're wearing those white uniforms, like the guy who gave them water and the guy who took away their dirty dishes. And one has a cook's hat on. And these people are all lined up and they're clapping. Al waves to them as he drives out of the lot. Wilma says she turns around and they're clapping until she can't see them anymore. When they reached the highway, Al turned to her and said, 'I didn't think the tip was *that* good.'"

Dorothy said to me, "You know, my brother got served in a segregated restaurant in Alabama once."

"How'd he manage that?"

"He wrapped a torn sheet around his head and talked with a phony accent. They thought he was from some foreign country."

After that, every time I passed my bread down the line,

I imagined the kitchen help in Arkansas clapping in the parking lot while Wilma and Al drove by, waving like visiting dignitaries. Sometimes, I pictured Al wearing a turban.

* * *

Nearly everyone on the cellblock had made a friend through their toilet vent. I thought about trying to contact whoever was on the other side of the wall, but what would I say? What if he wanted to thank me for the bread, as if it had been my genius that had gotten it over to him? That would be embarrassing. I'd have to tell him it wasn't even my idea. "If you're eating some of my bread," I'd say, "you're welcome." Maybe I could offer to mark the slices I sent down in some way. "Yeah, good idea," he'd say. "A hacksaw in the middle would be nice."

Kitty told us Tyrell was in the punishment cell for slow hoeing. "They beat him up and threw him back there naked. They sleep on steel, you know."

Sheila said, "What's Tyrell's crime?"

"He's supposed to have stolen a chicken from the woman he worked for. He says he didn't."

"Isn't there some joke about everybody in prison being framed?" said Hannah.

"Even if Tyrell took that chicken," said Kitty, "he doesn't deserve to be locked up for six years."

"For stealing a chicken?" I said.

"They get them for infractions," said Kitty. "Extend their sentences. Like now, he's in the punishment cells. They'll probably give him another year or two. That way they keep the farm going with free labor."

"The guy behind me won't talk," said Hannah. "I've tried to get him to say something but he won't."

Cora Lee said, "The guy behind me's named Wendell

and he's in here because he didn't get up quick enough at the end of dinner. He was trying to grab an extra bite."

"They're starving," said Kitty. "Even when they're not in the punishment cells. They're working on a farm and they're starving. Isn't that sweet?"

* * *

That night the voice I'd been hearing in the distance came loud and clear through the vent. "Y'all in there, I know. I can hear y'all."

I froze on the way down from a sit-up. Dorothy continued reading the Bible.

"Hey, y'all. Can you hear me?"

I scooted over to the toilet. "Hey! What's your name?"

"Ellis Lee. Know what I has here?"

"No. What've you got?"

"A mighty big chocolate cake. Four layers. My sister bring it with some peaches and cherries. My, my, that cake be tasting so good. And those peaches be juicy and sweet, running all down my chin."

I turned to Dorothy and said, "I hope it's true that what goes around, comes around. He's making me awful hungry.

"Last week I got me these cookies. You like chocolate cookies?"

"I do." I looked over at Dorothy again and mouthed, "Is he bonkers, do you think?"

She shrugged.

"Trouble is, I gots a bad spot in my mouth. Sometime, feel like it's sticking a knife up in there. But everybody need to take the bad with the good. That's just the way it be. My sister the best cook in five counties. I'm sore missing her chitlins. They so tasty, one bite feel like going home."

"Well, that's nice," I said.

"How old are you?"

"Eighteen," I lied.

"Well, little girl, welcome to the big house."

"How old are you?"

"On Friday, January 13, I turned twenty-three." He sounded as if he were pronouncing sentence on himself.

"You superstitious, Ellis?"

"Not sure I know what that mean."

"Black cats. Walking under ladders. Stuff like that. You believe bad things happen to people on Friday the 13th?"

"Bad thing happen to me."

"What was that?"

"Got caught."

* * *

I sat up and blinked. The glaring lights were hard to squeeze out, even harder to let back in. Dorothy's outline was a blur against the sick green of the wall.

"What's going on?" I rubbed my eyes. From the other end of the cellblock, I heard a moan.

Cora Lee called out, "We need to get Buckerfield down here. Thomasine says she's got appendicitis. She's been sick since day before yesterday and it's getting real bad."

"Use your toothbrushes to scrape the bars," yelled Kitty. I clambered down and grabbed my toothbrush off the sink. Dorothy was already pulling hers across the cell door. The block echoed with the noise we were making and with our cries of "Jai-ler! Jai-ler! Jai-ler!"

After about twenty minutes, my throat was raw, but I didn't hear anything from Mrs. Buckerfield's end of the cellblock until hours later when she opened the gate and yelled, "Cut out that goddamned caterwauling!"

Cora Lee called, "It's Thomasine. She needs a doctor."

Mrs. Buckerfield waddled down the cellblock. I pressed against the bars to see. She stopped in front of Thomasine's cell. Thomasine must've had her face buried in her mattress, her moaning sounded muffled. The matron didn't look at her for more than two seconds before she turned and left the block without a word.

I stood there, stunned, but Kitty, her voice threadbare, raised it again and we all joined in: "Jai-ler! Jai-ler! Jai-ler! Jai-ler!"

Sometime toward dawn we stopped chanting "Jailer" and started shrieking, "Help!" The gate at the end of our block creaked open and Mrs. Buckerfield shouted, "Cut out that mess! And I mean it!" The door slammed.

Light was bleeding up into the inky blue visible in the high windows when we heard, "Man coming!" He shuffled past, carrying a doctor's satchel. Again I ground my cheek into the bars and saw him standing several feet in front of Thomasine's cell. "You'll be all right," he said, and shambled back toward the gate, pursued by our insults: "Call yourself a doctor! Come back here! She could die! Come back, you fiend! Don't go—!" The gate slammed. Thomasine whimpered and grew still.

* * *

By the time the breakfast cart came through, Thomasine seemed to be all right. "Chronic," she explained. "I should've had it out a year ago but I'm scared to go under the knife."

If that appendix had burst, we couldn't have saved her. We could've bawled until our throats were bleeding. She'd be dead. Mrs. Buckerfield would call for someone to take the body away and that would be that—just like the stabbed man in the alley and the boy grabbed off of T.J.'s porch in Indiana. Just like Emmett Till. Being young didn't mean you got to go on living.

"I heard y'all," Ellis said that night.

"Do you know what happened?"

"Ain't no secrets in here."

So he must know who we were, even though he never asked about us. "She could've died, Ellis. These people can do any damned thing they want."

"You don't want'a use words like that, little girl. Give peoples the wrong idea."

From behind the Bible, Dorothy said, "He's right."

"Ellis, don't you hear what I'm saying? There's nothing stopping these people from killing us if they want to!" I thought I heard him chuckle. "It's not funny."

"Naw. It ain't funny."

"It has to make you mad too."

"What you going to do, little girl? You going to stomp your foot? That's just the way things is."

11

ELLIS LEE CALLED through the vent. He had a new shipment of goodies.

"Hey! I'm over here looking forward to molasses and grits for breakfast, Ellis—I hate molasses and I have no idea what grits are. And here you are, talking about strawberry cake. I wish you had a strawberry cake but, even if you did, I wouldn't want to hear about it. Tonight they gave us some awful meat, I don't know what it was. I'm sorry to be saying this because I know you must be hungry but, believe me, you guys are getting the best off our trays."

He didn't seem to have heard what I said. "Strawberries just right about now."

"I guess so. But I'm trying to tell you, it makes me hungry to think about them."

"But I likes to talk about them."

I rolled my eyes. "Ellis. Have you ever thought of using your time in prison to learn a trade?"

"Say what?"

"You know, carpenter, plumber—don't they have some kind of training program here?"

"Naw, nothing like that."

"Well, what work did you do before you went to punishment?"

"Used to be a cook."

"That's a trade."

"Too hot."

"Parchman must have some kind of library, don't they? Something. What about learning a new trade from a book?"

Behind me, Dorothy was talking to Hannah. "He doesn't listen to anybody, he never has."

Ellis Lee said, "I don't believe they got no library."

I scrunched down closer to the vent. "Your sister could bring you some books. They'd let you have those, right? At least, once you get out of punishment. Is there any job in particular that interests you? Some subject you liked in school?"

"You ever hear tell of something call a persomon?"

"Persimmon?"

"That's it. I likes to pick those after it get cold. You pick them in August, they be too tart."

"I've never had one. But, seriously. What're you going to do for a living when you get out if you don't want to be a cook again?" He didn't answer. "How long do you have to go?"

"To go?"

I remembered the courtroom in Jackson. Maybe he didn't know how much time they gave him. "I mean before they release you."

He didn't say anything. I began to think he'd left the vent. "Ellis?"

"Thing is, little girl, I can't read. Never learned."

"Oh, jeez, I'm sorry. I didn't realize—"

"Tell you what though. I misses my onliest brother. Ain't seen him in about three years. He live up in Colfax. It be too far for him to come visit me."

I looked back at Dorothy, who was smoothing her hair. "I don't know," she was saying. "After all, who am I?"

"Feel like I's awful tired tonight, little girl. I be saying goodnight now."

Dorothy said, "His mother has season tickets to the opera. She took me to hear Beverly Sills. She was Rosina in *The Barber of Seville*. I was so happy, I thought I'd faint."

I climbed into my bunk and hugged my knees. For the first time since the day I got there, I felt I truly couldn't bear to be in that cell.

12

IOLA BROUGHT our breakfast trays. She lingered at the bars, her hard brown eyes glittering. "Some of those mens be in trouble," she said, glancing over her shoulder to the end of the corridor where someone stood with the food cart, probably watching her. "They in the hole."

Dorothy got up. "Who?"

Iola shrugged. "Whole bunch of them thought they was smart. They mighty hot now cause Captain Ray got that air conditioner turned off and it be so many of them in there, they can't hardly catch they breath. I heard some of them be crying."

"Who?" demanded Dorothy, grabbing the bars. "David Hanover? Is he one?"

And Chris. Was he one too? Oh, I hoped he wasn't jammed in there, trying to get a breath of air.

Iola assessed Dorothy with a sleepy grin. "He your man?"

"Is he one of them? Is he locked in the hole?"

Iola smiled and moved on. Dorothy shrieked after her: "Iola, please! Just ask. Please! Just ask!" But the trusty had gone. The doors at the end of our corridor banged shut.

Most of that day, Dorothy lay quite still. The cellblock talked about the men in solitary, and Sheila suggested a hunger strike.

"But what about the bread?" said Kitty. "Are we going to stop giving it to the guys in back of us?"

"If we take it," said Sheila, "it's going to look awful suspicious."

Cora Lee said, "Captain Ray will say we're just pretending not to eat."

"But I hate to stop giving that bread out. Those guys need it."

"They'll be out of there in ten days at most," said Hannah. "They won't die."

"Is that true?" I asked Dorothy. "Are those guys only in for ten days?"

"I don't know."

How long had I been hearing Ellis Lee's voice? Longer than that, I was sure.

I called out, "The guy behind me—I think he's been there for at least a couple of weeks."

"Even if they're in longer," said Hannah, "believe me, they won't starve to death. Parchman's been doing this for years. I think they know how to keep unpaid help alive."

Cora Lee said, "We have to support our men."

It was agreed then that we'd explain to the men in the punishment cells why we couldn't give them any bread for a few days.

"So it's just symbolic," said Kitty. "I mean, if it's only a couple of days—"

"Just until they let the men out," said Cora Lee. "Once

we hear they've done that, we can end the strike."

Dorothy groaned, "A couple of days." No one heard her but me.

"We need a spokesperson," said Thomasine. "Somebody's got to explain to the Captain we're on a hunger strike."

I looked at Dorothy. If they made her spokeswoman, she might pull herself together. "I nominate Dorothy," I hollered.

"Okay," said Kitty. "Anybody else want to nominate someone?"

"Dorothy's fine with me," said Thomasine.

Several shouts of "Me too" echoed through the cellblock. "Well, Dorothy," Kitty called, "looks like you're it."

Dorothy's eyes opened. I thought she might say no but she dragged herself off her bunk and went to the bars. "Okay," she said. And that was all.

* * *

Captain Ray stood before us in his immaculate prison uniform. "So y'all on a hunger strike." He didn't look upset. Behind him the trusties lugged in buckets and mops. "Well, I guess afore y'all get weak from not eating, we better get this here cell block spanky clean."

I said to Dorothy, "Shouldn't we protest?"

She got up. "What's the point? The cell's dirty. Somebody ought to clean it up."

A trusty handed in a mop and Dorothy took it. The trusties continued up the line, giving out pails and mops.

The Freedom Riders began to sing:

Oh freedom, oh freedom, oh freedom over me
And before I'll be a slave I'll be buried in a my grave
And go home to my Lord and be free

I took the rag and started wiping out the sink. But I was mad. We didn't know what was going on with the men. I felt positive Chris wouldn't be mopping and singing after hearing we'd all been crowded into a single cell.

> *No more mourning, no more mourning,*
> *No more mourning over me*
> *And before I'd be a slave, I'll be buried in a my grave*
> *And go home to my Lord and be free*

"Stop it!" Captain Ray's shout bounced off our concrete walls and our steel bunks. "Shut up! Stop that noise!"

Dorothy called out, "Okay, everybody. Quiet."

Every mouth closed. I glared at Dorothy. The Captain came to a halt in front of our cell, his hands on his hips. He was smirking. His eyes connected with mine. I think, one second before I acted, he suspected trouble was coming. I heard my voice, at first thin, but shot directly at Captain Ray and growing stronger:

> *No more crying, no more crying,*
> *No more crying over me*

Before I finished the third "no more crying," everyone on the cellblock started singing. Dorothy looked at me and shook her head, but she joined the singing. We kept it up while the trusties carted out our mattresses, leaving us the cold perforated steel trays the men in the punishment cells had to sleep on.

Captain Ray strutted up and down before us, but his triumph had soured. He called out to us, "When y'all gets ready to apologize, then maybe we'll see about them mattresses." He stopped in front of our cell again, but this time he didn't look at me. His weak chin sank to his chest and he lifted mournful eyes to Dorothy. I waited. There was no time to vote. As our spokeswoman, she had the authority to apologize on our behalf. Captain Ray stood ready to forgive us. "Just say you sorry and I'll have them trusties bring y'all's mattresses right on back."

The cellblock grew hushed as Dorothy gazed out at Captain Ray. I wanted to shout, "Don't say anything!" but I had to accept that it was up to her. She looked small and thin, like a narrow bundle of straw, her hair standing on end, and yet she seemed surprisingly dignified in her striped skirt and soiled blouse.

"We have nothing to apologize for, Captain Ray," she said, and the cellblock erupted in a wild cheer. I moved closer to her as the Captain stomped away. When he was gone, I leaned over and kissed her cheek. She didn't object.

* * *

Iola came to collect the untouched trays. She paused again in front of Dorothy, who stared at her with hollow eyes. "Somebody," said Iola, "done fainted. I don't know who, but that's what I heard. He must be awful sick, they begging to be let out."

I said, "Iola, you're lying. They must've been taken out hours ago and you know it."

She smiled. "Believe what you wants to believe, I don't care."

Dorothy climbed back into her bunk.

"Go away," I told Iola.

I tried to reason with Dorothy. She listened with eyes the color of egg yolk spotted with blood. "Iola hates us," I pointed out. "Captain Ray puts her up to tormenting you. Think about it." Her eyes slid over toward me. "I mean, come on, they have to be out already. Ray wouldn't take a chance on somebody getting seriously hurt. He knows the world's watching the Freedom Riders."

"If the world worried about the Freedom Riders, we wouldn't be locked up in here. Now go away and leave me alone."

I looked around the tiny cell. "Care to suggest a practical destination?"

She turned away from me and pulled her knees up.

* * *

Ellis Lee had told me there were no secrets in the prison. So he had to know if the men were out. If he said they were, Dorothy would listen.

I called several times but he didn't answer. I sat on the floor, wondering if he'd been taken out of punishment. Then I heard the grind of his cell door opening and the clang of it shutting. He'd been taken out of his cell and now he was back. What had they taken him out for, I wondered. A shower? Did the men over there get showers? It didn't seem likely.

"Ellis!" I called.

"Leave me be, little girl. I's mighty low today."

* * *

CORE's lawyer came to see us, a dark man with brows that looked like caterpillars nesting above his distant, bottomless eyes. He stood outside the cell. "It's fairly certain," he told Dorothy, "that they are out. Captain Ray claims they are out. However, he refuses to allow me an interview with the men. This concerns me, as it might mean they are suffering some ill effects." He waited while Dorothy hiccupped through a sob. "We are filing a writ and we expect to gain access later today or early tomorrow."

"Tomorrow!"

His fingers smoothed his mustache, a pair of red parentheses punctuating his mouth. "Mrs. Hanover, I'm certain those men are no longer locked in solitary and that they were confined at most only a few hours. By giving in to your emotions, you are making things more difficult for yourself and your cellmate. Try to think of the effect you are having on her."

"Don't worry about me," I said from my bunk.

Dorothy stumbled to the sink where the toilet paper sat. She wiped her eyes and said, "I have a special reason to be concerned about David. He's not as well as he looks. Right now he could be in need of medical attention."

The lawyer flipped through the papers on his clipboard. "I have no medical notation on David Hanover. Is there something I ought to be made aware of?"

She hesitated. "No. No, he wouldn't—Please, if you could only find something out for me. If I only knew he was back in his cell—"

"As soon as I have any information, I will certainly see that it gets to you as quickly as possible."

"Why were they locked in solitary?" I asked him.

"To make them sorry they came, I presume." He moistened his fingertip on a dart-shaped pink tongue and again attacked the clipboard. "Turner," he reminded himself. "Yes. The Justice Department has decided against filing your case."

Although I knew, I said, "What does that mean?"

"They don't intend to pursue charges against you, although from what I have learned, they would be within their rights. I met with them for several hours last week. It was not time well spent, I might add. You're the first Freedom Rider to violate your oath."

"Within their rights? Those men hit me and pulled my hair!"

He blinked. "I'm sorry. When you volunteered was it not made clear to you that such a thing might happen?"

I flushed. "I didn't know I'd be treated like a piece of meat on some kind of auction block."

He stuffed paperwork into his briefcase. "I don't see the relevance."

"The relevance is we're fighting for human dignity, Mr.— " I stopped. I didn't know his name.

"Pelton."

"Mr. Pelton."

"Unless there's more—?"

"I guess there's no point in saying more."

"Not unless it involves your legal situation."

"I guess Mr. Pelton doesn't realize the world revolves around you," said Dorothy, as the lawyer moved down the cellblock.

I pressed my forehead into the cool bars. "Okay, Dorothy. Fine. I admit it. I should never have done what I did. Happy?" I looked over at her thin face. She'd lost weight and she hadn't carried enough flesh to begin with. "You didn't want to do this," I said, suddenly certain this was true.

"No," she said. "I didn't."

* * *

That evening Iola told us that one of the men got very sick and the others were begging for him to be taken out. Dorothy screamed, "Get him out of there!" She had to know Iola didn't have the authority to free her husband, but she kept screaming anyway. "You have to get him out!" Dorothy slid to the floor.

An odd smile stretched Iola's mouth. "How you know it's your man?" she said to the back of Dorothy's head. "I ain't said who."

"So why don't you?" I snapped, trying to help my cellmate to her feet, but she stayed crumpled at the foot of our cell door.

Iola glanced behind her. "I don't know who."

"It's him!" sobbed Dorothy. "Don't you think I know? They hit him last month—they hit him and hit him—he's epileptic! God damn it, he could die!" She whipped around, her face contorted. "Damn you, you bitch!"

I was shocked. Iola didn't react but I was scared. Suppose Dorothy didn't pull out of this? The doctor wouldn't touch her. The matron wouldn't care. I'd have to deal with her all on my own. Growing up, I'd had way too much experience taking care of a crazed woman. I didn't want to go through that again, if I could avoid it.

Iola studied her, huge mahogany eyes as blank as they'd been when she watched Mrs. Buckerfield jam her claw into my rear end. "I know one thing," she said with a crafty smile. "This ain't your man. Can't be your man." Dorothy turned away from her again, the angular line of one hip jutting out. "Well, if you ain't interested," said the trusty, looking around. "He's a honky," she said at last. But Dorothy ignored her and Iola gave up and went away.

Somehow I got Dorothy into her bunk and I climbed onto the steel beside her, trying to hold onto some part of her that wasn't razor-like.

"He's going to die," Dorothy moaned.

"Remember what you told me, Dorothy? About not freaking myself out? That was good advice."

"He could swallow his tongue."

"He's not in there. Iola's playing you. Come on, don't let her. This isn't like you."

"If she's just playing me, why did she say he wasn't my husband? I need somebody to tell me he's all right," she wailed. "I have to know!"

Hannah began to yell for Mrs. Buckerfield. I didn't know what we'd do if she came—ask her to let the men out? Ask her to tell Dorothy they were out? The rest of the cellblock started shouting too. I untangled myself from Dorothy and joined in, even though I couldn't see what could possibly come of it.

She lay on her steel bunk, knees pulled into her chest, her head thrown back, wailing. I drew my toothbrush across the cell door, counting with the others: "One – two – three – jai-ler!"

Eventually the door at the end of the cellblock ground open and we heard the flat slap of Mrs. Buckerfield's slippers. She stopped in front of our cell and waited for the electric door to slide open.

I said, "Dorothy thinks her husband's locked up in solitary." Mrs. Buckerfield ignored me. "She needs somebody to tell her those men are all right. You know they are. Just tell her."

The matron batted me aside and reached in with one massive arm, yanking Dorothy out of her bunk and shaking her in her blouse until I thought her spine would crack.

"Shut your trap!" She dropped Dorothy on the floor like a discarded sock. "That goes for every one of y'all," she flung at us before the corridor gate slammed shut.

Looking like a coffee-colored Raggedy Ann, Dorothy slumped on the floor. But she had grown quiet. I crouched next to her and she sank into me. I put my arm around her and we huddled together without speaking. Toward morning she turned and looked at me, seemingly with astonishment, like someone waking up in a strange place. But the expression was fleeting, and she chased it with a weak smile. "Thank you," she said, clambering to her feet. "He didn't want anyone to know." I smiled as if I understood. She went back to her bunk. For a minute or two I didn't move, afraid of shattering her calm. But her breathing evened out and soon I saw she was asleep.

13

I KEPT TRYING to talk to Ellis Lee, but the few times he bothered to answer me, he only said, "Leave me be, little girl. I'm hurting bad." Every time he didn't answer me, I worried he'd been sent back to the Farm and I'd never get to speak to him again, never find a way to make up for humiliating him by making him admit to me that he couldn't read.

Hoping he was listening, I told him we'd been on a hunger strike. Captain Ray had finally reported that all the men were out, perhaps hoping this would inspire us to kiss and make up. "That's why we couldn't send any bread over for a couple of days. But you're going to get some today. It's over."

"Leave me be," he said, and so, heart sore, I did.

* * *

After breakfast, Captain Ray would come in to ask if we were ready to apologize. Dorothy, like a queen receiving a diplomat from a country with nothing to offer, would give him a brief audience. I waited for her to say something about David and the men who'd been in solitary. She never did.

101

Stoic in her bare feet and sagging skirt, she'd tell him we had nothing to apologize for and Captain Ray would grimace as if her rejection actually hurt his feelings.

Dorothy passed every day studying the Bible and sleeping, or staring at the underside of my bunk. Once she said, "Why doesn't the lawyer come?" and I said, "I don't know," and she said, "Oh," as if she'd already lost interest in the question. Sometimes she began to talk as if we'd been in the middle of a conversation that had been interrupted and she was picking up where we'd left off: "He planted vegetables last year. They died," Or, "My mother liked him. She wanted me to marry him." These non sequiturs poured out of her now and then while I was trying to get Ellis Lee to talk to me, so that I would hear his dead voice telling me to go away on one side and Dorothy's curious eruptions on the other.

* * *

Iola brought a note with breakfast. Dorothy, as usual, lay numb on her bunk. Iola hissed, "Come on, girl, you gonna want to see this." Then she nodded at me. "They all right," she said, and hurried off to finish delivering breakfast.

"Who're you kidding?" I shouted after her. "We knew they were all right days ago."

The note, on folded toilet paper, lay beneath Dorothy's biscuits. She did nothing for several minutes and I wondered if she'd heard Iola. But then she pulled herself into a sitting position on the edge of the steel bed, which, with its deep lip, couldn't be comfortable. Even so, she stayed there for a while, bent over her lap, her rumpled hair making it impossible to see her face.

At last she took the note from her tray and hunched beneath my bunk, reading. I removed my tray from the slot. Normally I'd sit with her to eat. But I didn't want to intrude so

I set my tray on the top bunk and started climbing up after it. I saw we had some dry scrambled eggs so it looked like I'd get something more than chicory coffee this morning.

"Want to see it?" she said.

I nodded and she handed the note to me. It was unsigned.

I had a small seizure in solitary. Please remain calm. My release is three days away. I'll see a doctor when I get to Jackson.

"Well," I said, "it sounds like he's okay."

"He wants to be a martyr for the cause."

"He's getting out in three days, right? And he says he'll see a doctor."

She placed her arm over her face. "He lost an eye last year," she said. "I think he was glad."

I folded the note and put it on her bunk because she didn't seem to have any interest in taking it. "Is it true he's white?"

She took her arm down. "Why?"

"I don't know."

"What difference does It make?" She covered her face again. "So what if he is," she murmured in such a small voice, I almost didn't catch it.

* * *

"Misery come calling," Ellis Lee explained, "best leave somebody be." His sister, he said, brought no more baskets. "Told her don't be bringing me no more of that mess. Just fattening me up, that's all. I don't know why she come at all. I done told her a hundred times, just leave me be."

"You'll get out of that cell pretty soon," I said. "They can't punish you forever, right? Things will look better when you're out. You'll see."

103

"Time for me to go to sleep."

* * *

About two weeks before our group was due to get out, I received a letter from my mother. That was a bad sign. Rita didn't write letters—they weren't immediate enough for her. I set it down on my bunk and it sat there like a snake, waiting to strike. Dorothy was dozing, the Bible on her lap. I thought about waking her up and asking her to read the letter for me. It was stupid but I thought if I watched her face, I'd know how bad the news was. The thing was, I hadn't heard from T.J. since that one note the censors just about erased. I told myself they weren't letting more of my grandmother's "dangerous" messages through, that was all. Maybe they knew about her background.

The idea was ludicrous, of course, although T.J., in her post-Communist Party paranoia, would've endorsed it.

When I couldn't stand it anymore, I opened the note and was immediately sorry I had.

> *Dear Jeri:*
> *T.J. had a heart attack. She fell and got a concussion. Some ribs broke and one leg too. Doc says its osteo something like that. That's why her bones got broke. The doc says shell get better but they keep doing tests and I don't know what else their going to find. You need to come. Shes in St. Marys.*
> *Love, Rita*

The lawyer must've tried to get into the cellblock to tell us the men were all right, but we hadn't seen him. I'd have to beg the matron to call him. "You should've thought about that before y'all came down here making trouble," she'd say. "I ain't nobody's servant," she told anyone who asked for

anything except sanitary napkins or toilet paper. Even if I did
see the lawyer, it might take four or five days to file whatever
it was he had to file to get me out. If he was willing to do me
any favors. I was, after all, the only Freedom Rider to break
my promise to be nonviolent.

I could hear Mrs. Buckerfield in the shower, treating
us to another verse of *My Man Done Gone Away*. After she
turned off the water, the scent of lilac cologne would throb
down the cellblock, mingling with the stink of our unwashed
perspiration. I didn't envy her the cheap scent but I did envy
her regular bathing. Twice a week we were permitted a one-
minute rendezvous with soap the color and consistency of
adobe.

Supper came but I stayed in my bunk. Dorothy sent our
bread down without comment. The trusties collected the trays
and went away in a barrage of clanging. I lay there picturing
T.J. trapped in bed, with Rita hovering over her.

My mother had written something about what more the
doctors might find. What more? If I thought she wrote those
words to needle me, I'd never forgive her. But I knew she
didn't mean anything. Life and my mother just happened,
she plotted against it no more than it plotted against her. That
much I had come to understand about her when T.J. never
could. To T.J., Rita was the author of her own losses, someone
who deserved to be a victim when my grandmother had no use
even for those victims who didn't deserve what happened to
them. T.J. was a woman of bootstraps. When I was eleven and
heard her going on about how people made their own luck, I
told her that if you actually tried to pull yourself up by your
bootstraps, you'd fall over. She came close to slapping me.

She and I had been locked in a battle of obstinacy ever
since I could recall. Once, when I was about six, I'd insisted
she had to hold my hand crossing the street. "Why?" she

snapped. "Does it make you walk better?" I could still feel the malice that inched through me as my grandmother stood there uncertainly, wanting her hand to belong to her but uneasy with denying my claim to it.

She'd squeezed my fingers until I cried as she dragged me across the intersection.

* * *

At the vent I could hear Ellis Lee tapping. On my bunk, I rolled toward the wall, my hands over my ears. Dorothy called up, "There's your boyfriend." Ellis Lee tapped again. "You've been pestering the poor man to death, but now that he wants to talk, you don't want to talk. Stop sulking and answer him."

"I'm not sulking."

"Little girl, I know you there."

"I don't know what you're doing. But you better answer him before one of the guards comes around."

I pulled myself up and dangled my feet off the edge of my bunk.

"My sister come by today. She promise me a new basket tomorrow but can't get no plums. They all gone. You hear me, little girl?"

I sighed, and reluctantly climbed down to the floor. Squatting next to the vent, I said only, "Yeah."

"I be sorriest to miss them wild plums I used to get down by Colfax. I ask Yolanda would she make me some plum jam but she say she really ain't got the time."

I rubbed my forehead, my temples throbbing. I couldn't bear ten more seconds of this babble. "You'll live," I snapped.

"Say what?"

"Never mind." When Ellis finally got bored with describing mountains of fantasy food, maybe I could get

Mrs. Buckerfeld to bring me two aspirin. *Sure,* I thought. *Fat chance.*

"She did bring some cookies today, even in spite of I told her not to. Chocolate chip. She say the smell of chocolate make me change my mind in a big hurry. Sure enough did."

I leaned my forehead on the toilet seat, massaging my temples. "Let's stop pretending, okay, Ellis? Nobody gets cookies in here. I don't even remember what a cookie looks like." Behind me, Dorothy issued a low, indecipherable murmur. "You do know who we are over here, right?" No sound came from his side.

Every nerve in my body thrummed. That was one way men like Ellis Lee wound up in prison for their whole lives. They lived in a world of make-believe. Sure, reality had to be hard for him, even horrible, but he couldn't change anything by pretending. Instead of thinking about the future, Ellis Lee was over there chewing on imaginary baked goods. Well, he wasn't going to tell me any more tales, not with T.J. maybe dying. I wasn't going to hear that mess tonight. *She could already be dead, for all I knew. The censor might be blacking out the telegram right now.*

"Well? Do you know who we are?"

"I done told you, ain't no secrets in here."

"So?"

"Does y'all know who I is?"

I looked over at Dorothy. She grimaced. "If he says Napoleon, I think I'm moving to another cell."

My head felt like splintering glass. "I give up. Who are you?"

"I's one of the mens on death row."

With my hand over my mouth, I shot backward as if I'd been struck. It couldn't be true, could it? Those were punishment cells.

But his sister's visits, the fruit and cookies and cakes—they were real.

All the things I'd ever said to him stung me like needles: *Study for a new career*? I slipped down the wall. *You'll live*? Had I actually said that? *And how much time do you have to go*? How much time *did* he have left? I couldn't ask. He was only twenty-three, much younger today than he'd seemed to me the day before. I began to weep.

"You hear what I say, little girl?"

"We heard you," Dorothy called out. I lowered my face to my knees.

Ellis Lee asked, "What about her?"

"She can't talk. She's crying."

I didn't know if he heard her, but he grew quiet. After a long while Dorothy fell asleep, but I stayed close to the vent, my head on my arms, my tears now and then splashing into tiny pools on the concrete floor.

14

I SAT ON the floor wondering if I should ask the lawyer to get me out sooner. I couldn't make up my mind to do it. T.J. needed me but I couldn't see turning my back on Ellis Lee, not after he'd told me he was going to die. What had he done to get himself on death row? Oh, that was a good one. A black man about to be put to death in Mississippi and I was wondering what *he'd* done. What did Emmett Till do? No, I had to find out if there was some way to save him. T.J. might need me but she wasn't alone and the only ones who could save her were the doctors.

I wondered how they killed people at Parchman. Electricity? Gas? Then it hit me. I didn't know when they were going to do it. He'd been down for several days. Maybe his date was close. Maybe one night I'd be lying on my steel bunk and I'd see the lights flicker and that would be the end of Ellis Lee.

* * *

I heard clicking in the sink and craned my neck to see a

fat brown bug come out of the drain and crawl up the porcelain wall. He kept falling backward—that was the clicking—but then he'd just start over again. I named him Sisyphus. What kept him at it, time after time? Was it too awful in the drain? Maybe there were other bugs down there with whom he didn't wish to associate. Sisyphus was still climbing and falling around midnight when the heavy tread of footsteps on the cellblock behind us brought me out of my fog.

No one moved through the penitentiary at night. The racket of slamming doors and rolling carts died some time after the final meal, the late silence broken only by Mrs. Buckerfield's shower song. When the door crashed shut behind her, we heard nothing more until the breakfast cart. But something was happening back there now. They executed people at midnight, didn't they? Maybe the guards had come to escort Ellis Lee to the death chamber—to kill him in the first minute of the day the judge had set for him to die. Maybe I'd never hear his voice again.

A cell door scraped. There was some kind of scuffle back there and angry shouts. It was Ellis, I was sure it was Ellis. He was about to die and I was over here locked up in a concrete box with no way on earth to help him. They were going to kill him. I wanted to call out but my throat closed. I couldn't breathe.

Then I heard water. Someone screeched. I bolted to my feet and shook Dorothy.

"Wake up, wake up!" Her eyes opened. "Listen!" She stared at me, sleepy and puzzled.

"What's that?" she said.

"I think they're running the shower behind us." *That was good, wasn't it? They wouldn't give Ellis Lee a shower and then take him to the death chamber, would they?*

Shrieks rattled the vent. Dorothy sighed, shook her head,

and sank back down. "They're beating them."

I shook her again. "Don't go to sleep."

"I'm awake," she said from under the arm thrown over her face.

Everyone was awake now. I don't know how I could tell but I could. We were all listening. A scream. Then a thud. Then another scream. Someone begging. *Please please naw, naw.* I yelled into the vent, "Stop it! Stop it!" Dorothy said, "Cut that out!" but the other Freedom Riders were now bellowing into their vents as well.

"Take it easy, little sister. It'll be all right." It was his sweet voice, low and soft. I couldn't have heard it if I hadn't been pasted to the vent. "I's all right."

I didn't dare answer Ellis. What if they heard me? They'd beat him. But right after he spoke to me, I heard his cell door open—I knew it was his, it was so loud in the vent. He said, "Y'all gonna do me?" I thought he laughed. I turned in agony to Dorothy. Her arm was still over her face. "They're going to beat Ellis—"

She said tiredly, "They like to beat people. It's what they do."

Thud, scream, thud, scream—it went on and on. I counted the thuds—one, two, five, seven, ten. Fifteen. Nineteen. Finally, silence. The pounding water stopped pounding, the screaming died away, and I heard a cell door slam, footsteps leaving. Captain Ray had finished his night's work.

I called out, "Ellis Lee?" There was no answer. Again I called.

Dorothy said, "Leave him alone, hasn't he had enough trouble for one night?"

I sat there for a minute, wanting at least to hear his voice, to know that he could speak. I whispered, "Just mumble if you're all right."

He said nothing.

At the end of our cellblock, the gate ground open. My heart stuck in my throat. Dorothy sat up. She looked nervous. I was terrified. Captain Ray, his uniform fresh, his shoes winking in the fluorescent glare, strode in, surrounded by grinning trusties with handcuffs and clubs and what I supposed were brass knuckles. They stood in a line, performers taking a bow.

Captain Ray was a little boy at Christmas, his eyes alight. From behind his back, he slowly withdrew a small net-wrapped bundle, its cargo bashed to crumbs. I know he spoke. I heard only the clicking of the water bug scaling my sink. Click, click, click. In the Captain's doughy face the slashed mouth kept opening and shutting. A roar filled my head. I looked from one trusty to another. The one standing next to Captain Ray stroked his brass knuckles fondly.

The cell doors slid open and two trusties began to drag something in. A mattress. Dorothy got up from her bunk and stood back. A second mattress started in, but I threw myself at it, pushing the trusty backward, screaming, "No! No! No!" The Captain stood outside the bars, his face pink and radiant. I raised my hand to the trusty, who backed off, rolling his eyes toward the Captain.

Ray cleaned his fingernails with a nail file. He gestured with it toward the end of the cellblock. "Got a hole down there waiting for you, Geraldine."

They could kill Ellis Lee, Thomasine, Dorothy's husband—they could even kill me. What good would it do to keep that mattress out of my cell? I stood back and the trusty heaved it up to the top bunk.

The Captain and his helpers went away. I moved to the sink and scooped the water bug out. My eyes were full of tears. The bug landed near one naked toe but I flung the Bible down and then I stepped on it to make sure that dirty brown bug was crunched into a million pieces.

* * *

"Little girl?"

I grabbed the vent. "Are you okay?"

Dorothy snorted, but Ellis said, "Take more'n a little whupping to do me." But his voice was raw from screaming.

"Why did they beat you?"

"They always be wanting to do me like that. I be used to it. No sense in y'all worrying yourselves 'bout none of this mess. Get some sleep now."

I couldn't sleep. If I started to drift off, Ellis Lee bucked wildly in the electric chair.

"What did you do?"

"Don't ask what you don't want'a hear."

"Do you have a lawyer?"

"Get away, please, just get on away from me now."

* * *

"Geraldine Turner." Mrs. Buckerfield hung from my cage door, a slab of beef in a rayon dress. She looked me up and down, making a face. "That's a nigger name if I ever heard one," she said. "How come you supposed to be white? You don't look white."

"After seeing white people in Mississippi, I hope I'm not white."

"Think you're pretty damned funny, don't you?"

I just looked at her.

"Good riddance to bad rubbish, I say. You and that spokeswoman person—y'all be getting out tomorrow."

When Mrs. Buckerfield had gone, Dorothy uttered a small joyless, "Hallelujah."

"Tomorrow."

"You sound like getting out of here's a funeral."

"It is a funeral. What about Ellis Lee? What's going to happen to him?"

"Same thing that would happen to him if you didn't get out tomorrow."

"I need to talk to him."

"He told you to leave him alone."

"I have to say goodbye—I have to tell him I'm not going to forget him." Rita's letter stuck out of my shirt pocket but Dorothy didn't seem to notice it, or at least she showed no curiosity about it.

She stood at the sink, washing her hands. "If that man wasn't going to die, what do you think he'd be doing for the next forty years? Black in Mississippi. Uneducated. Illiterate. It's not much of a life."

"You mean it doesn't matter if he dies because he's not your husband."

She pursed her lips. "I guess I do mean that. My husband works for the good of communities. His life carries more weight because he's important to more people than himself."

"Or you."

"Or even me."

"I forgot. You didn't want to come down here. You don't really care what happens to any of these people."

"I care. But my job is supporting my husband and the work he does. I can't let myself be distracted by the Ellis Lees of this earth."

* * *

"Ellis, listen, I'm getting out tomorrow."

"I knows it."

"I want to help you."

"Little sister, you can't help me. Go on home and behave

114

yourself."

"Do you have a lawyer?"

"Lawyer ain't going to do me no good."

"I know you didn't get a fair trial. We can appeal your case, Ellis. But I have to know what you did."

"Leave me be, little girl. Y'all can't do nothing to change what is."

"When—when are they—when is it supposed to happen?" He didn't answer. "All right, but I'm going to help you, Ellis, I swear it. I'm not going to leave here and just forget you. Do you hear me?"

He didn't answer.

* * *

I climbed up to my bunk and closed my eyes, the sound of Dorothy's low snoring lulling me toward sleep. But when I started drifting off, my eyes flew open. They might come for him any time. That very night could be the one. I looked at the lights, terrified I might see them flicker. Then I climbed down and sat by the vent, trying very hard to hear something moving in his cell.

"Ellis," I whispered, "just tell me you're still alive. Please!"

"I ain't," he said.

15

WE GOT OUT at the Jackson train station on Mill Street. Chris took out a piece of paper and studied it. "We should head north."

Thomasine pointed. "Look there. That's giving us something to think about, especially in this town."

I squinted up. A sign hung on the wall of a triangular building:

Eternity Where Will You Spend It

Chris smiled. "Got any plans?" I was confused by his question and I must've shown it. "For eternity," he said.

"I can't even figure out what to do with the rest of today."

Behind us, I heard the harsh bark of Ned's laughter. I suspected he was trying to impress Sheila. I said, "How'd it go in there? I heard about what happened to you—you were in that crowded cell, right?"

He nodded. "I've had more fun listening to my dad's sermons, but the time passed. I'm glad it's over."

"Have you heard from your dad?"

"Not possible. He doesn't know where I am."

I stared. "But why not?"

"Because we haven't spoken in five years. Let's stop here," Chris said, pointing to a corner grocer. "I need cigarettes."

* * *

CORE was the kitchen of a minister's home, located next to a small, one-story church with a sign on the lawn: **ALL ARE WELCOME**. The yellow house was tiny, immaculate, and its porch had recently been painted lime green. Some scraggly red geraniums struggled out of a flower pot next to the door sill. We reached the stoop just as the clouds began to leak. I was surprised to see Paul Warren open the door.

He led us into the kitchen, where the table held stacks of flyers. In one corner, boxes rose nearly to the ceiling. Paul was stuffing these flyers into the stove's firebox. Now and then he stopped to stir a pot of some sort of stew bubbling on top of the firebox. The temperature could've been 120 degrees in that room.

"This stew isn't for us," he apologized, placing the wooden spoon in the ceramic hand of a grinning chef. "It's for the church supper tonight. The Reverend asked me to keep an eye on it."

The kitchen was crammed with boxes. Paul had thrust the window all the way up, but no air stirred. I felt soggy.

"I'm here to organize the departures," he said. "Then I go to New Orleans."

"Why're you burning flyers?" said Chris.

"Reverend Harrison doesn't have space to store them. Speaking of storage, your suitcases are in the bedroom."

I looked around. "I need to make a phone call, Paul. It's long distance, but I can get the charges from the operator."

Paul indicated the phone in the hallway. "Go ahead, but make it quick." He stooped to look out the window. "The rain's stopped. Would you guys start stapling the leaflets in the hall. They're for the march tonight. You can use the porch, it's pretty crowded in here."

Chris said, "Not to mention, hot," as he cut in front of me and grabbed two boxes near the telephone table. He turned back to the kitchen. "What march?"

I turned my back to them and gave the operator the number of T.J.'s apartment. Rita answered after three rings. She sounded vague, as always, and a little pressured. But she wasn't flying high and she wasn't catatonic. Miraculously, she seemed to be straddling the normally elusive middle-ground. It made me think there might actually be a God.

"I'm going back to Frisco tonight," she said. "This dump depresses me."

I could picture my mother slung sideways on T.J.'s drab olive chair with its one wobbly arm. Her bony ankles would be sliding in and out of her Capri pants as she wiggled. Rita was always wiggling.

"What about T.J.?"

"That hospital is a bummer, Jeri, know what I mean? But with you coming home, she'll be okay. I told her I'm going, it's all fine with her. There isn't that much wrong with her at this point, you know what I mean? A few broken bones. She has to be careful, not get excited. Worst thing is you wouldn't believe the shit they give her to eat. Well, you know T.J. She ain't eating it. I tried arguing with her but that's a waste of hot air, truthfully." Without the words *truthfully* and *know what I mean,* I don't think my mother could have completed a thought.

I remembered her draped over that same armchair years before, her eyes guarding the door, waiting for T.J. to come home. She had chain-smoked her way through a pack of Pall Malls and drank cup after cup of the coffee I made, everything she said punctuated by *truthfully* and *know what I mean?*, which, being nine years old, I mostly didn't. Rita often showed up unannounced, but T.J. had called from work and I'd told her my mother was there. "She needs to go back to San Francisco," T.J. growled. I didn't answer because Rita was a few feet away.

I'd turned my back and hunched my shoulders, as if that could keep my mother from knowing. "Are you coming?" I whispered into the phone.

"I got stuff to do after work," T.J. said, and hung up.

T.J. hadn't shown up until long after Rita had left, going back to her little apartment in San Francisco. That was before she returned to Los Angeles and moved in ten blocks from us, which was before she went back again to San Francisco, to the little apartment, inexplicably (from her perspective) still available. I'd seen it once and I couldn't imagine anyone in her right mind renting it.

In those years, I'd often thought of my mother as a moth, flitting from one end of California to the other, blown by the winds of whimsy and kept aloft only by disability checks that T.J. pursued and directed to my mother's most recent location.

"She waited for you!" I followed my grandmother through the flat.

"I know how she waits," T.J. had snapped. "She's like rain hanging around. She would've been the same if I'd come home. The difference would've been I'd of had to put up with it. She drips all over me, I can't stand it."

I shifted the phone on my shoulder and glanced into the kitchen. Paul was stuffing the firebox and stirring the stew. How could he stand the heat? "What if I don't come back right away? Who's going to look after her?"

"Well," my mother sighed, "you know how she gets. I wouldn't want to be the one to tell her you wasn't coming."

"I'll try to catch a plane in a couple of days. Can't you hold on until then?"

"I'd like to, but you know, the niggers are taking over my place, just thick as flies in that building. Truthfully. A friend's going by checking every day but still I can't be sure, you know what I mean? One of these days they're going to bust in and clean me out."

"You haven't got anything in that flat worth taking. And they're called Negroes. Think you can pronounce that?" Her world was too disjointed for my mother to have made a connection between my going to jail in the South and her fretting about "niggers" stealing her pathetic belongings.

"Well, I'm sorry," she said. "I didn't know you'd gotten so sensitive."

Chris smiled at me from the porch. He probably could see this was rough going. "Tell me how she's really doing, Rita."

"She's got tubes, you know, her arm, and even in her—well, you know what I mean—she can't even go to the bathroom."

Looking at her mother, at my grandmother, Rita could not glue the parts into a whole. She tended to view everybody in her life in pieces. She'd been eager to fix my breasts up in a training bra when they were buds. "What're they in training for?" T.J. demanded. "I'd rather Jeri had untrained boobs."

"What do you do, Rita? I mean, when you're with her."

"I just hang around. Just be there. It helps people, you know, having somebody there." That stung. "A couple of times I read the paper to her, but she don't seem to want to hear it."

"Has she asked about me?"

"I try and get her to think about other things, truthfully, but it's like she thinks you did something to her, like this whole thing was just a way to hurt her. I don't truthfully know what to say to her."

I cut her off before she could say "truthfully" again. "I need you to stay with her, Rita. Until I get there. There's something I have to do here but she shouldn't be alone."

Her sigh swirled through the receiver. "Hey, Geraldine." The sound of my name coming out of her mouth startled me. Now and then, although rarely, my mother would say *Jeri* or *Jer*—a tick of the clock in which my existence solidified in her consciousness before dissolving once more—but she'd never called me *Geraldine*. "I have things to do too, sugar."

"Just a few days," I pleaded.

She sighed. "Just a few days," she echoed. "That's all I can give you. The niggers—"

"Oh, god, thank you, thank you. Just a couple of days. That's all I need." I closed my eyes and prayed craziness wouldn't send her reeling out of Los Angeles onto some mission no one else could comprehend.

When I hung up, it occurred to me she'd never asked me what I needed to do. But then I scolded myself: *She's crazy, remember?*

* * *

Through the window I spotted a police car at the curb. The men inside were sitting back, hats tilted forward, apparently sleeping. I went into the kitchen.

"I was just telling the girls about the sleeping arrangements. Just one warning: Don't bother to unpack. You won't have time in the morning. Your ride will get you at six."

Chris came in behind me. "Everything all right?" He

pulled me back into the hallway. "You look upset."

"I have to make another call." I went back to the phone bench, Paul's frown pursuing me. I realized I'd forgotten to ask the operator to give me the charges. Well, I'd give Paul a dollar. The call couldn't have been more than that. "This one's local," I said.

I half-expected the number not to be in the phonebook, but it was there. Before I dialed I inhaled several times, praying that my voice wouldn't break or turn funny on me. What if they wanted to know why I was interested? The man who answered listened to my story without speaking. Several times I felt I'd finished, but he said nothing so I tacked on some more. Finally, I asked, "Does the NAACP know about Ellis Lee?"

"We know about him."

"Okay," I said slowly. "What're you doing for him?"

"Nothing."

"But why?"

"What makes you think this is any of your business?"

"He's my business because he's my friend. And he's your business because he's a Negro in trouble. If that doesn't make it your business, maybe you need to change the name of your organization."

"Excuse me, someone's at the door."

"Wait! Please. Just tell me what he did."

"If he's a friend of yours, ask him."

The phone went dead in my hand. I sat there, puffing, my teeth clenched. Then I grabbed the directory again, nearly ripping the pages.

This time a woman answered. She said Mr. Logan had gone out, that he wasn't expected back at all for several days. I told her, "That's not true, I just talked to him," and she hung up too.

My hands shook as I thumbed through several more pages of the directory. City Hall. Records Office. I dialed and was transferred through three offices before I reached the County Courthouse.

"Well, what date did you have in mind exactly? I'm sure I can't read your mind."

"Couldn't you go by the name?"

"Honey chile, I'd be delighted to accommodate you, I'm sure, but the fact is, we go by dates and if you don't even know the judge or the lawyer or the date—"

"But how many people can Mississippi possibly have on death row?"

"Now," she said, "when you ask rude questions, I can't help you."

The dial tone buzzed in my ear. I took another breath and picked up the phonebook again. My forehead was smeared with sweat and a dark stain was growing down the front of my shirt. A receptionist, sounding bored, answered.

"I'm awful sorry but Mr. Pelton has a conference in New York City. I expect he'll be back come Tuesday but not before then. Is there something I can do?"

"Yes," I said, clutching at this first offer, "I want the court records on Ellis Lee. He's at Parchman."

"Court records," she drawled, "are expensive."

"How expensive?"

"It depends on the length, I can't tell you a flat figure."

I exhaled loudly. "Okay, then just tell me how I can get a look at them."

"Well, you can't. That's the thing. Unless they have some kind of appeal going, they don't bother about transcribing them."

"This is a capital case," I said. "An appeal would've been automatic."

"Not in Mississippi. But if you tell me when the trial took place, I'll find out what I can. I mean, when Mr. Pelton calls, I'll ask if it's all right, but I'm sure—"

"I don't know when."

"Oh. Well, just tell me who the attorney of record is. We can find out from him."

"That's what I hoped to find out from Mr. Pelton." I turned toward the back of the house to bend over and wipe my face with my T-shirt.

"I'm sorry, but I really don't see what I can do. When Mr. Pelton comes back, he can call up the prison and they might tell him something. I'll ask him, if you want."

On the porch I could see Chris still watching me as he and Sheila stapled flyers, doing my share of the work.

"What's going on, Jeri?"

"Nothing," I said because there was too much to say.

He took hold of my shoulders and drew me out onto the porch. The cops turned to look as Sheila and Ned moved inside to give us some space. "Come on, what's going on? Talk to me."

"He's going to die."

"Who's going to die?"

"Will you find out why he won't help me? Mr. Logan. He's head of the Jackson NAACP and he won't talk to me."

"Talk to you about what?"

"Ellis Lee. He's on death row. Oh, Chris, they beat him up on account of the bread—he kept telling me his sister brought him all this food and I—I didn't believe him. But it was true."

"Slow down. I can't follow you." Chris sat on the railing. As I told him about Ellis Lee and the night Captain Ray beat him and the men in the punishment cells, his jaw clenched. "Fuckers," he said under his breath. "Poor kid."

I didn't know whether he meant Ellis or me. "He'll talk to you— Mr. Logan. I'm sure he'll talk to you."

Chris went back in the house but he came out again too quickly.

"He says CORE's trying to bust the NAACP."

"Even if that's true, so what?"

"About Ellis Lee, Logan says quote forget him. Unquote. I get the impression your man is not regarded as a model of injustice in the state of Mississippi."

"Did you ask him what Ellis Lee's crime is supposed to be?"

"Couldn't. He said his piece about CORE and hung up." The street wavered like a mirage, heat like fumes in the air. "I know how you feel, Jeri. But you really don't know anything about this guy. Maybe he deserves to die."

"No," I said.

"Well, I think you should give a little more weight to what Logan says. He knows more about the situation than you do."

"He's the head of the NAACP, hanging up on someone asking him about justice for a Negro. I don't care what he says. I know Ellis. He didn't talk to him. I did."

16

PAUL CLAPPED his hands for attention. He had reassumed that officious expression he'd worn throughout the workshop sessions. "Please keep in mind that these are Christian families. They may not say anything to you but they'll notice everything you do. We had one girl who sorted her dirty laundry on the kitchen table. Needless to say, that family has never housed another Freedom Rider."

My thoughts were whirling. Ellis Lee. T.J. I didn't have any money. What should I do first? What could I do? If not to the NAACP, where could I go for help? Paul was going to hand me a plane ticket, tomorrow morning somebody would dump me at the airport, and that would be it. Ellis Lee would die.

Paul nudged my elbow and said, "Okay, let's go."

* * *

The screen wasn't latched and behind it the front door stood open, so Paul herded us in, calling out, "Hello! Mrs. Lymon!" His voice was lost in a barrage of gunfire and hoofbeats. Two little boys and a pudgy girl of about fourteen sprawled on the floor of the darkened living room, all eyes riveted on the television as we picked our way through. They didn't acknowledge us, even as we filed past the screen. Through another door we found ourselves in a bright kitchen where Mrs. Lymon greeted us, getting up from her cup of coffee and whatever else had been holding her attention. She was a tea-colored woman with straightened brown hair that was straggling out of the ponytail she'd stuffed it into. She looked tired.

"Maybe y'all like to sit out in the garden."

Chris squeezed my arm. "Chin up," he murmured. "See you at the rally." This only vaguely registered. I didn't know what rally he meant.

Mrs. Lymon took Thomasine and me outside and we sat down at a metal table beneath a metal umbrella. When I thought no one was looking, I wiped my wet eyes with the back of my hand. Around us there was nothing but naked red dirt, freshly raked, surrounded by a green picket fence.

"The ground's poisoned," said Mrs. Lymon matter-of-factly. "Can't have nothing growing 'cause of the pollen. Mr. Lymon has the worst allergies, y'all can't believe how bad it gets for him."

The chubby girl slipped from behind the kitchen door and squinted at us, one hand shading her eyes. "Y'all Freedom Riders?"

It was rather like being asked if we were members of Jesse James' gang. I thought the girl might want to come down the stairs and touch our sleeves. But she only continued to gaze at us. "Once," said Mrs. Lymon, "I planted squash. Only two or three at the back of the lot. Poor Mr. Lymon like to died."

I glanced around at the neighbors' yards, filled with grass

and weeds and flowers.

"What's it like in jail?" asked the girl, still standing at the top of the steps.

Nearby I could see the two boys creeping toward us, their fingers at the ready: "Gotcha! Ya yeller-bellied coward!"

Thomasine said, "Jail's okay. Nothing to do most of the time."

"Some jails," said the girl, pressing one nostril to sniff, "they makes you work. Parchman Farm. Peoples work there."

Thomasine sniffed too. "We didn't."

Mrs. Lymon inched around her daughter and came down to place two glasses of pink lemonade on the chipped white paint of the table. Shreds of pulp gleamed iridescently on the surface of the juice. I took a sip. It was warm and chewy.

I thought of Ellis Lee and of his strawberries.

Mrs. Lymon said, "Sweet Pea, go see is those beans sticking. I forgot to check on them."

Sweet Pea ignored her. "I wanted to go on them Freedom Rides," she said. "My papa wouldn't let me."

"You have to be at least eighteen," said Thomasine.

Coming down the steps at last, her skirt billowing in damp, wrinkled swells as she moved, Sweet Pea trailed her fingers along the railing. "I could go downtown tomorrow. Or today. Right this minute. Go down there and walk into Walgreen's Drugstore, big as you please. I could sit down and say, 'One cold glass of CoCola, if y'all don't mind.'" She giggled, standing a few feet from us, her ravaged skin like yellowing plastic over good furniture. I saw a pretty girl under that bad skin. "Bang!" She whirled and fired her index finger at one of her brothers who snuck around the corner of the house. He pitched forward on his face, into the poisoned dirt. Sweet Pea looked indulgently back at us. "I don't need be no eighteen to do that."

"I better go see about them beans," said Mrs. Lymon.

"I'm going tonight," said Sweet Pea, as her mother scurried up the steps. "I'm going on that torchlight march and I'm going into that church and I hope somebody bombs it because I think the funniest thing in the world would be to die in church, right here in my home town—where my papa says I'm safe!" She plopped herself down in her mother's chair and looked from Thomasine to me. "Did they strip y'all naked? I hear they do that."

I liked Sweet Pea.

"You shouldn't disrespect your mama when she asks you to do something," Thomasine pointed out.

When I was little and whining about my mother's spells, T.J. would tell me, "You don't need to respect her, Jeri. Just accept her for who she is. Your mother didn't decide to go crazy as a way to make life hard on you."

"You're a fine one to talk," I'd snapped one morning over my Post Toasties. "I remember plenty of times *you* wouldn't talk to her."

T.J. had dropped her head, looking down into her coffee, and I understood I'd hurt her feelings. "Some days," she'd murmured, "are rougher than others, Jeri. You'll understand when you're older."

I should've telephoned the hospital, should've talked to my grandmother. Most likely, Rita would forget to mention my call. I said, "Can I use your phone?"

"We don't got one."

"Well, do you know where's the closest one?"

"Back where y'all came from, I expect. There's one in Otto's—that's the luncheonette over next to the church."

Mrs. Lyman was nowhere to be seen. I passed through the living room where the television bellowed at the empty floor. The Lone Ranger's nasal voice trailed me out the door: "That's right, Tonto. He's a good man."

* * *

When I got to Otto's Cafe, I saw Chris and Paul sitting together. Paul said, "What're you doing here?"

"I have to make a phone call."

"Sit down."

"After I speak with my grandmother."

"I need to talk with you."

"And I need to know if my grandmother's okay. I promise I'll sit down with you after that."

I stood at the pay phone with my shoulders hunched, rummaging through my coin purse. The operator at the hospital switchboard explained T.J. didn't have an extension in her room.

"Ring the floor, then, please."

The floor nurse repeated that T.J. had no phone.

"I'm her granddaughter. Please. It's urgent. I've been in jai—away. I couldn't call her until now."

"Really, it's not possible."

"But there has to be a way. Could you wheel her out to the desk?"

"On what? Her bed?"

"I don't know—a wheelchair—can't she sit up?"

"Her condition is stable, but she's not ready for a wheelchair."

"Oh, please, Miss—I'm sorry. What's your name?"

"Rowens."

"Miss Rowens, I really need to hear my grandmother's voice. She's the person who raised me and I just found out about her heart attack."

"I offered to have a phone placed in her room, but her

daughter didn't seem to think it was necessary."

"What about the intercom?"

"I can't do that."

"I'm begging you. I—I don't know what's happening to her. It's been over a month. Please, won't you get her on the intercom, at least for a minute or two?"

The nurse sighed. "Hang on."

The operator asked for fifteen cents. I riffled the bottom of my purse. Empty. "Chris!" I called, looking over my shoulder. "Could you loan me a little change? I've run out." He came over, digging in his pockets. A moment later I heard a faint voice through the receiver.

"Hmmm?"

I shouted, "T.J., it's Jeri. Are you okay? Are you going to be all right?"

"What—? Jeri—?"

"I'm calling from Mississippi. I just got out of Parchman. Listen, I'll be home in a couple of days."

"No!"

Chris had gone back to the table. He and Paul watched me, expressionless. I turned to the wall.

T.J. said, "I need you here now. Not in a couple of days. You've been gone long enough."

It was T.J., the same rough burred voice, yet it wasn't her at all. She'd never needed me. "Is Rita there?"

"I'm here."

The nurse broke in, "I have to close this off. I'm sorry. If you want a telephone installed, I'll arrange it."

I looked at the nickels and dimes in the palm of my hand and said, "Install it."

"We don't need a phone," snapped T.J. "Come home, Jer. Today. You're out, right? It's over."

"I can't, T.J. Not yet."

131

"I've got to close this off," said the nurse.

"Please deposit another fifteen cents," said the operator.

"I'll call back, T.J. I promise."

"No!"

That was the last word I heard before the nurse shut down our connection and the operator followed suit.

"So what's wrong?" asked Paul.

"I'm sure you heard me. My grandmother had a heart attack." I placed the leftover change in front of Chris. "I appreciate the loan. I'll pay you back."

"CORE can arrange for you to fly home tonight. You can see your grandmother first thing in the morning."

"I can't fly home tonight, Paul."

"I can't allow you to stay."

I looked at Chris. "You told him."

Paul wiped the rim of his coffee cup with a paper napkin. "If your grandmother's ill, you need to go home."

"Is that what you would have told me before I came on the Freedom Rides?"

He drew his lips back into that censorious look that made me feel cranky. "We aren't here to save one man. We're here to improve life for all Negroes."

"You mean, all those who aren't condemned to die."

"People are counting on us, Jeri, believe it or not. If we screw this up, we're throwing away the biggest opportunity to come along in a century."

"I'm not screwing anything up, Paul. It's just like you harping on Communism. You make a big deal over things that don't matter."

"By things that matter, I presume you're thinking about this man on death row."

"Ellis Lee, yes. That's his name."

"Jeri, the people who support us don't want to be

associated with a man like that."

"What do you mean, *a man like that*? He's a human being."

"He's on death row. The NAACP has no interest in him. That's enough for me."

"Do you know what he did, Paul?"

"No, Jeri. CORE has no interest. We need to stay focused on what we came down here to do."

"Do you agree with him, Chris?"

He slid his eyes away from me. "Partly."

"Okay, fine. But I'm not giving up and I'm not going home until I find a way to help Ellis Lee."

"What about your grandmother? It sounds like she needs you."

"That's for me to worry about, not you and not Paul either."

Chris caught up with me outside. "What's your commitment here, Jeri? A convict you talked to a couple of times?"

From across the street, three small children gaped at us. "That's just it, Chris. I talked to him."

"So the hell with what anybody else thinks, right? Because *you talked to him*."

"Wait a minute," I said, and stepped back inside the diner. "Pelton's not going to help me, is he, Paul?"

He drew in a long breath and blew it out like a ribbon of smoke. "No. He isn't."

"Could you reach him, if you wanted to?"

Chris and Paul exchanged unreadable glances. "Where're you going with this, Jeri?"

"If Pelton won't help, he can give me the name of an attorney in Jackson who will." They looked at each other blankly. "Well, can't he?"

"Have you got money for a lawyer?"

"If no one will do it pro bono, I'll get the money somehow."

"Nobody's doing pro bono work for a Negro on Mississippi's death row, not for this guy anyway."

"But I thought a capital crime meant a person was entitled to free legal counsel. Somebody ought to be working on Ellis Lee's case."

"Maybe someone is," said Chris, looking to Paul.

But Paul shook his head.

"Isn't that the law? I thought it was in the Constitution—due process, or something," I said.

"You may have noticed, Jeri. Mississippi doesn't have a lot of respect for the Constitution."

I turned to Chris. He'd had a good job and, whenever he paid for something, I noticed a lot of cash in his wallet. "Please," I said. "If you have it. I'll pay you back. Maybe you could loan me enough to get somebody started and I could find the rest someplace else." This was nonsense. I had no idea where I could find the kind of money any lawyer would need to defend Ellis Lee all the way to the Supreme Court. And I was pretty sure it would have to go there, if he was going to have a chance of overturning his death sentence.

Chris grimaced, but said to Paul, "Do you know anybody?"

"I can give her a name. I doubt it'll do any good."

"Give it to her."

Paul took a battered black notebook from his shirt pocket and wet his finger to leaf through it. Then he took out a pen and started writing on a napkin. "Amos Starkweather. His office is on Cassidy Street."

I took the napkin. "Thank you. Now I have to make another call."

Chris reached in his pocket and dragged out a nickel.

"Make the appointment for early tomorrow, Jeri," said Paul. "Tomorrow afternoon, you fly home."

* * *

Sweet Pea's father didn't come home before we left for the march. Mrs. Lymon didn't try to stop her daughter from coming with us, even helped her to find a flashlight, which Sweet Pea played wildly over the purpling Jackson streets as she and Thomasine and I found our way to the beginning of the march.

"You're going to wear out the battery," warned Thomasine.

Sweet Pea turned the beam on her own face, "The betta to see you with, my deah," she giggled. She leapt ahead of us down the street, forcing us to hurry behind her wavering trail of light.

When we neared the corner, I saw hundreds of beams of light. Most of the people carrying them wore loose white robes, like choir robes. It was as if we'd joined a group of angels. They were singing:

> Paul and Silas were bound in jail
> Had no money for to go their bail
> Keep your eyes on the prize
> Hold on, hold on
> Hold on, Hold on
> Keep your eyes on the prize
> Hold on, Hold on

I kept staring up at the speckled darkness as it swooped behind the rooftops, the trails of light flickering across the sky, and I thought to myself, *Paul's right about some things. This* is *bigger than one man. T.J. always said I liked the odds when it was me against the world, and maybe that's all that's*

*making me so sure everybody else is wrong about Ellis Lee.
Here I am going into battle against an evil giant, but what if
he's the evil giant?*

> *We're gonna ride for civil rights,*
> *We're gonna ride for both black and white.*
> *Keep your eyes on the prize*
> *Hold on, hold on*

Sweet Pea's face kept being washed by bursts of radiance.
There was nothing silly about her now. She sang and clutched
her flashlight between her breasts. Even Thomasine seemed
caught up, lovely in the swirl of light. Behind us more people
joined the march, their flashlights lacing the blackness in
which we marched.

I knew the Jackson police stood by with dogs and
truncheons, eager to punish us. I knew, too, that along the
darkened edges of our march, Klansmen and members of the
White Citizens Council watched from the shadows, hating us.
It struck me that their hatred corrupted the air, and our songs
could keep us from breathing in that filth.

When we entered the church, we blinked in the abrupt
glare from overhead lights and from police lights trained on
the windows and doors. Our mood shifted from somber to
festive. A handsome minister, his looks spoiled only slightly
by his slick processed hair, stood on the stage, clapping his
hands and leading our singing.

> *Ain't gonna let nobody*
> *Turn me round,*
> *Turn me round, turn me round*
> *Ain't gonna let nobody*
> *Turn me round,*
> *Walking and a-talking,*
> *Talking and a-walking,*
> *Walking into freedom land!*

One woman leaned across Sweet Pea and took Thomasine's hand and mine in each of her own. "God bless you," she said.

"Stand up! Stand up! Let's get us a look at these here freedom fighters!"

Sweet Pea pushed at my elbow. "He be talking about y'all."

Thomasine hesitantly rose. I saw Chris across the room, and Ned. The only other white face in the church belonged to Paul. He was on the stage sitting behind the good-looking man who urged us up. "I'm Reverend Carroll. And y'all best introduce yourselves because these good people wants to go on and give y'all the biggest hand anybody ever got. These young people come to us straight from Parchman Farm, ladies and gentlemen! Give them a big big hand."

We stood there, our heads bowed in posed modesty, listening to the applause, to the shouts of "Hallelujah!" And I wished I could tell everyone in that church about Ellis Lee. Maybe somebody would want to save him.

* * *

Thomasine climbed the stairs of the Lyman's house. Sweet Pea hung back, but the door opened and Mr. Lyman, outlined by the television's light, said, "Sweet Pea? Come inside now."

She made a face but trudged up the steps. "I'll be in there in a minute, Mr. Lymon," I called. He nodded and closed the door.

Chris said, "I'll come by at eight-thirty tomorrow morning. We can walk over to Starkweather's office together. I'll get the directions from Paul. But after you see him, we're going to New Orleans and we're taking the next flight home. Okay?"

"Let's wait and see what Starkweather says."

"Whatever Starkweather says. If you don't leave when Paul tells you to, Jeri, he doesn't have to give you a ticket home. You'll be stuck in Jackson."

A police car cruised slowly past, but it didn't stop.

"I'll help you tomorrow," Chris said. "But that's it." The police car made a U-turn and now drew up to the curb next to us.

"Y'all got a problem?"

"No, sir," said Chris. "Just saying goodnight."

"Seems to be taking quite a while."

I turned slightly away. "Don't say *sir* to him."

"Shut up," said Chris under his breath. "Go inside."

"I won't."

"Damn it. Do it before you get both of us in real trouble."

"All right, all right."

Sweet Pea was at the curtains. "That's Sam Weaver," she said as I came in. "That man be after every colored girl in Jackson."

"Sweet Pea!" Mrs. Lymon stopped rocking in the corner. In the dimness I could see the outline of half a sweater across her lap, knitting needles like crossed swords in front of her.

Mr. Lymon stretched across the sofa. His snores wove through the ricochet of gunfire on the television. On the floor his sons lay on their stomachs, chins on their fists, their eyes glued on Lorne Greene and Pernell Roberts killing desperados.

"Well, he is. He come after me. He say why didn't I take a little ride in his cruiser, and I was going to go 'cause I thought it'd be fun, but Rennel come up, saying my Mama wanted me. You didn't, though. Rennel told me her sister one time did it with him."

138

"Sweet Pea!"

Through the window I could see Chris only as a dark shape moving away from the patrol car. I bit my thumbnail. "Will they follow him?"

Sweet Pea peered out the window again. I felt her tense up, almost felt the decision as she made it, a current rippling between us. Even so I was startled when she threw open the door and raced down the stairs.

Sweet Pea's mother dropped her knitting and stumbled over the motionless bodies of her sons, crying, "Stop! Where you going?" But she halted in the open doorway, her breath caught like a hooked fish. She peered out into the darkness, whispering, "Oh my lord." Below us Sweet Pea approached the patrol car.

From the top of the porch I watched, as undecided as Sweet Pea's mother.

"Should we wake up Mr. Lymon?"

"No," she gasped. "No."

The wrinkled skirt spread over Sweet Pea's substantial bottom as she leaned over, placing her elbows on the car door. One cop was half-hidden in the dark corner, smoking, staring out the window in the direction Chris had taken.

Sweet Pea's laughter floated up to us. Beside me, Mrs. Lymon seemed suspended against the air, leaning toward her daughter as if the force of wind currents alone held her back. I didn't want to go down there, to suggest I, too, was available, not even to keep those men away from Chris. If one of them touched me, I didn't know what I might do. I glanced at Mrs. Lymon. Her hands were knotted in her skirt. I went out the door and descended the steps.

Sweet Pea was saying, "One hundred and twenty-six dollars and eighty-three cents." The patrolman held a pencil stub and had twisted away from her to take advantage of the street light.

"Move out of my light," he ordered Sweet Pea, but I was the one standing in his light. He turned his head and our eyes locked in the kind of staring contest I hadn't had since grammar school. I looked away first. Sweet Pea's eyes danced over me. She seemed to feel we shared a secret. I couldn't think what it was. Her betrayal of the Movement had stunned me.

"Let me go on back inside now, y'all."

"Talk to you later," said the cop, pocketing his notebook and releasing the handbrake.

When he was out of sight, Sweet Pea burst out laughing. "Miss Osgood—she clean house for the sheriff's wife," she said, grinning at me. "And she tell that white lady everything she know. Everybody know. And Miss Osgood was sitting right there in the front row when they called the collection plate. And Reverend Carroll gonna put the count in his newsletter anyways. But that cracker fool wrote it all down, like I told him something."

From the top of the stairs, Mrs. Lymon watched her daughter, her hands worrying each other. I couldn't see her face. Sweet Pea was still laughing. "When I was a baby girl playing Secret Agent, I wrote down better stuff 'n that. In invisible ink, too."

"Oh, Sweet Pea," Mrs. Lymon said softly, "why did you tell Captain Weaver all that mess?" She stepped into the light from the street lamp. "Now he just be after you night and day."

"Don't call him captain, he ain't no captain," snapped Sweet Pea, but a defeated expression hovered over her face and I felt frightened for her. She rubbed her neck, peering down the street where the police car had gone. When she turned back to us, her cockiness had returned. "I knows how to play that man, I knows just what he's about, Mama." Mrs. Lymon dissolved back into the shadowy house where rifle fire still twanged and bullets sounded like miniature sirens. Through the open door I could see before the television set the outline of two small staggered profiles, as if one were the shadow of the other. Sweet Pea stared belligerently at me. "Don't you worry none. That man ain't going to get nothing from me."

What could I say? I looked away, overcome by her courage.

17

THE LAWYER'S ADDRESS led us to a small bungalow in a neighborhood of family homes. "You sure this is right?"

"Paul said Mr. Starkweather works out of his house."

"Really. Is he any good, do you think?"

Chris shrugged. "I'll wait here." He pulled out *To Kill a Mockingbird*.

"You kept it?"

"I never got to finish it and you didn't seem to like it much, so I figured you wouldn't mind."

"No, no," I said. "That's fine. But don't you want to come inside?"

"Uh uh. This is your battle, not mine." He sat down cross-legged behind a hedge that hid him from the street.

The front door opened before I had a chance to push the bell. A short dark man in horn-rimmed glasses stood behind the screen. "Mr. Starkweather?"

"Come in." He pressed himself against the wall to let me pass. Then he put his head out the door, looked over at Chris, and gave a quick nervous glance up and down the block.

"Back there," he told me, pointing to an open door. "Go on in." I stepped into a dim room furnished with a worn brown sofa and a plywood coffee table. In the corner a battered desk groaned under piles of books and papers. I sat on the couch. Mr. Starkweather brought a chair around from the other side of the desk and placed it so that it straddled the threshold between the hall and the room where I sat.

"Thanks for seeing me so quick."

He opened a notepad. "Do you want to tell me what this is about?"

"It's about a Negro named Ellis Lee who's on death row at Parchman. I'd like you to represent him."

Mr. Starkweather didn't write on his pad. He shook his head. "I'm afraid I can't help you."

"But why not?"

"I'm not qualified to litigate a capital case."

"But you're a lawyer."

He tapped the pad. "My area is insurance law. I do some civil rights work with CORE, but that's just because there aren't many lawyers in Jackson willing to get involved."

"Nobody's willing to get involved with Ellis Lee either. Even the NAACP. Mr. Logan hung up on me."

Mr. Starkweather went to the window and parted the curtain. He came back to his chair. "There might be grounds for appeal. Could be his attorney slept through the trial. That's not uncommon, in particular when the lawyer is paid by the state and his client is a Negro. But it wouldn't matter much in Mississippi. Our Supreme Court doesn't consider sleeping through evidence damaging to a defendant's rights."

"So you'll take his case?"

"No. As I said, I'm not qualified."

"Don't you think a condemned man would rather have an

unqualified lawyer than no lawyer at all?"

"You haven't said what he was condemned for."

"I don't know. He wouldn't tell me." He clicked his tongue. "You could find out, Mr. Starkweather. If you call up Mr. Logan, he'll tell you."

"Mr. Logan would not like it if I bothered him about a case he'd told you he wanted no part of. I'm sorry but I have to live and work in this community, Miss Turner."

"But you could go down to the Courthouse and find out there. Mr. Logan wouldn't have to know."

"Those proceedings won't have been transcribed." He got up. "Miss Turner, why don't you go on home and let these things take their course." He stooped and looked out the window again.

"I'm not going to do that, Mr. Starkweather. I'd be grateful if you could suggest a name or two, somebody you think is qualified."

He stood with his back to the window. "Let me be frank. Since Mr. Lee won't tell you his crime, I doubt he's authorized you to retain counsel on his behalf. Now if you'll excuse me—"

"So what you're telling me, Mr. Starkweather, is that it isn't only white racists who believe Negro lives are cheap."

I could see he wanted to scold me for that, but he bit back the words. Instead, he turned away, staring out through the curtain.

"I won't take the case—" he said without looking at me. "But I happen to know of a group of lawyers in Chicago who might. They worked a capital case in Alabama two years ago. I think I have one of their flyers." He went over to his desk and rummaged through the piles. "Here it is. Truth in Action Group." He handed a thin mimeographed brochure to me. "I warn you. I don't know what their political allegiances are but it wouldn't surprise me to learn they're Communists."

"I don't care about that. Not if they'll help Ellis."

Mr. Starkweather stood next to his desk, his hand on a file folder. His fingers seemed to be practicing piano scales on it. "The case would have to have some sort of community impact, I would think. At any rate, something about it would have to interest them."

I folded the pamphlet. "So I have to find out what Ellis was convicted of."

"I'm afraid so."

"But no one will talk—" I stopped. "Wait. I know."

Mr. Starkweather looked impatiently at the file he'd been tapping. "Miss Turner, please."

"I know. Just one more minute. Ellis told me he has a brother—who lives in . . . some place called Coleville, Colton—Colfax! That's it. Is there a Colfax, Mississippi?"

"About two hours north."

"Is it big?" He shook his head. "So I ought to be able to find him." I got up and stuck out my hand. Mr. Starkweather hesitated, but shook it.

As I stepped out onto his stoop, he stayed behind the screen. From there he offered me advice: "There's no shame in giving up on a hopeless cause, Miss Turner. Remember that."

* * *

"Where's the bus depot?"

Chris stood up, jamming my book into his back pocket. "Why?"

"Just tell me, okay?"

"I don't know where the bus depot is and I wouldn't tell you if I did. We've got someone waiting to drive us to New Orleans. Our flight is booked. We don't need a bus."

I started down the street. "I'm not going to New Orleans."

"Hey, wait a minute, Jeri. That wasn't our agreement."

I kept moving, walking backward. "I never agreed to anything, Chris. You and Paul did all the agreeing."

He caught up with me. "Where do you think you're going?"

"Colfax. I'm going to find Ellis Lee's brother."

"Jeri, you can't go traipsing off to—where's Colfax anyway?"

"Two hours north."

"Do you have money for a bus ticket?"

"I've got ten dollars. It's probably enough to get me there and back."

"And then?"

"Somehow I think getting home to L.A. will take care of itself."

He looked disgusted. "And to think I defended you when Paul called you a loose canon."

"Well, you shouldn't have defended me. I'm not grateful because then you snitched on me. I thought you were my friend, but I guess I was wrong about that."

"If I weren't your friend, I'd say go on to Colfax and get yourself lynched. It's no skin off my nose."

"But you don't care that Ellis Lee will be killed, and I do." I stopped. The truth was I was frightened of going to Colfax alone. I wished Chris would go with me, but I knew I didn't have a right to ask. "I can't live with myself if I turn my back on him, Chris. I've got to try and help him."

He squinted into the sun. "Remember when you said anybody could see how *To Kill a Mockingbird* was going to end—everybody living happily ever after?"

"So?"

"Atticus doesn't save the black man, Jeri."

"Okay, I'm a bad literary critic, but so what?"

"Lee himself refused to tell you what he did. Doesn't that set off alarms in your head? Nobody wants to tell you. And no one else thinks the man's worth saving. Can't you see how hopeless this is?"

"It probably is hopeless. But when those people took the bus to Anniston, it looked hopeless too. A lot of the time, this Movement looks hopeless. These people—" I waved my hand. "Some of them are ready to die to keep segregation, we know they're ready to kill for it. Should we give up?"

He was grinding his teeth. "I can't let you do this."

"Of course you can. You can't stop me." I started walking again, but he caught up.

"Come on," he said, taking my arm. "You win."

* * *

Chris adjusted the overhead mirror on the rental car. "You have an address for Ellis Lee's brother?"

"Don't worry, we'll find him. I have some ideas."

He threw the map down. It landed on my feet. "Your ideas will probably get us lynched."

"You know, Chris, you don't have to do this. I can still take the bus. Anyway, I don't understand why you had to rent this car."

He rolled down his window. "I don't intend to wait around at a bus stop while the Klan puts on its white sheets."

"But why not let *me* take the car and you can stay here?"

"Do you have a license?"

"No, but I took driver's ed."

He laughed.

"I don't want to feel responsible for whatever happens to

you," I said.

"You? Responsible for me?" He tossed his cigarette butt through the window. "I hope I get to laugh about that tomorrow."

* * *

"What did you tell Paul?"

"It's what he told me."

"Which was?"

"We're on our own." Chris lit another cigarette. "Somehow I wasn't surprised."

* * *

Colfax had no main street. In the center of town stood an old wooden church, its cross tilting. Further on we came on a rusting trailer, the roof holding up a sign with two pistols: **OLD WEST REALTY**. The trailer looked abandoned and so did the general store next to it.

"Over there," I pointed. "That gas station."

Chris made a U-turn and parked in front of the phone booth at the back of the station. He stayed in the car.

"Here's a listing for a Roberta Lee," I called out to him, dialing. The phone rang only once. The woman who answered was humble.

"Not related, ma'am, no. I's sorry."

I tried the number for a Walter Lee. Mrs. Walter answered. Her voice sounded white. "I never heard of no Ellis Lee," she snapped and cut the connection.

Next I tried the A.M.E. Zion Church, Rev. W. B. Foster.

Pastor Foster hung up when as I identified myself as a Freedom Rider.

I went back to the car. "I guess we better drive around until we see somebody to ask. Wait a minute!" I spotted two black children playing with sticks in a muddy puddle of water across the road.

"Hello! Hello!" I saw the children's eyes trying to get away from me. "I'm looking for Ellis Lee's family. You know who that is? His brother lives around here."

"Don't know nothing," said the boy. His sister began to cry. He patted her head a little too vigorously and she cried louder.

A small brown woman in a cotton shift came out of the house. She wore an apron and a lace cap. She didn't look at me but spoke to the children, "Y'all get out back, hear? Your daddy ain't gonna come fetch y'all till after supper."

"Hello."

She lowered her eyes. "Yes, ma'am." The children ran around the house.

"Do you know Ellis Lee's family?"

"Yes, ma'am."

My heart sped up. "Do you know where I can find them?"

"Yes, ma'am."

I waited. She kept her eyes on the ground. "Well, can you tell me where?"

"Yes, ma'am."

Chris yanked on my arm. "Get in the car. There's a white woman watching you from behind the curtain upstairs."

I slammed the car door. "Damn it. I thought sure she was going to tell me."

"She knew that woman was watching. Probably her employer."

Out on the highway, he said, "There has to be a Negro part of town. People there will know him. And I'd feel a lot safer surrounded by dark faces."

He turned onto an unpaved road. A few hundred yards in, I cried, "That's a store, Chris! See the Wonder Bread sign?"

In the front yard, three old men sat on crates, fanning themselves. They stopped talking when I got out of the car.

I walked past them. There was no point in asking old black men anything. They'd be scared to be seen talking to me.

The rusting screen door complained when I pushed it open. At first I couldn't see anything. The sour smelling room was nearly dark. I did see it wasn't really a store. It was the living room of a house, fitted out with shelves holding a few loaves of bread, some bottles of milk, and a case of soft drinks. From one murky corner, I heard a cough. It came out of what looked like a mound of rags.

"Hello? I'm trying to find the family of Ellis Lee."

Her face, lifted to a dusty sliver of light, looked like a shoe left out in the rain, stained and cracked, unevenly brown. She was chewing something. Eventually she nodded.

"He has a brother around here, right?"

She bent to spit a stream of black juice into a coffee can. "Who told you that?"

"Ellis Lee."

Her mouth gaped open, revealing no teeth. I couldn't tell if she was smiling. "Take care, ma'am, that boy carry the devil's mark."

"What mark?"

"Right here," she said, indicating her shoulder. "It look like the head of an old white snake. That mark be on him day he born." The scant light caught the tawny whites of her eyes. "You ever seen it?" she asked in a sly voice. I shook my head. "Well, missy, the minute I seen it, I knowed what it meant. And right away I said as how I believed it would come to be. And so it has."

"What came to be?" I demanded. I thought the sharpness of my tone might cow her but she looked back at me boldly.

"Do you know what he did? What put him on death row?"

"Put hisself there." She heaved herself up and the pile of rags fell around her. Her small head topped a massive body. From a distance of several feet I wrinkled my nose against the stench of her. She laughed, a dry cackling sound that crept up the back of my neck. "Alicia Ann!"

A child came to a doorway leading to the back of the house. She stared ahead with overlarge eyes, a spray of light exposing her milky pupils. Her wild hair seemed never to have been touched by a comb.

"Alicia Ann can't see," said the old woman unnecessarily. "But she know everything." She took the girl's dingy sleeve between two fingers. Alicia Ann's body swayed slightly. "Where Jurlean and them stay now?"

"Over to the old Watson place."

My pulse sped up. "Is Jurlean his brother?"

The old woman cackled. "Jurlean ain't nobody's brother. You talking about LeCharles Simpson. Go back out the highway and take the next left." She pointed with a bulb-knuckled finger. "About two miles. Magnolia Way. What's that address? Six sixteen?"

"No, Gramma. Six eighteen."

The old woman followed me out of the store but she was no longer interested in me. She gave Chris and the car a good long stare. One of the old men rose up and lifted a hand, as if to pluck at her attention, but she didn't see him. She turned without a word and disappeared, the ragged screen cracking shut behind her.

"I've got it!" I told Chris.

I could barely wait. In a few minutes I was finally going to know what Ellis Lee had done—if he'd done anything. He might be guilty only of being a black man in the South. Would his brother know if he was innocent? Ellis said his brother couldn't visit—it was too far. But Colfax couldn't be more than half an hour from Parchman. Maybe Ellis's brother didn't even know Ellis was there, waiting to die.

Chris reached over and touched my leg. "It's okay, Jeri. However this comes out, it's okay. Hold onto that."

* * *

A child of about four, eating ice cream and a baked potato, sat on the steps of the farmhouse at 618 Magnolia Drive. There was no farm, only a house in the middle of weedy fields. Wild mustard and dandelions carpeted the yard.

We parked under the beech tree shading the driveway.

I drew in my breath. "This is it." I felt as if my own hand hovered over the executioner's switch. Any minute now Ellis Lee could die.

But maybe he was dead already. I didn't even know that much.

Above us the branches hummed with sparrow chatter. The little girl kept munching on her potato.

"Is LeCharles Simpson here?"

Her pigtails didn't move when she shook her head. "He ain't here. No, ma'am." The bowl of ice cream jiggled between her plump knees.

From the house I could hear water draining out of a washing machine. "When's he coming back?"

The girl studied her half-eaten potato. "I don't know. No, ma'am, no, sir."

Chris came up behind me. "Is your mother here?"

I saw her then, behind the screen, a slight woman, fragile as milkweed. The door whined open. "Jurlean, take that mess inside and finish eating it in the kitchen."

"Mrs. Simpson?" asked Chris.

"I ain't no Mrs. Simpson."

"Do you know LeCharles Simpson? Ellis Lee's brother?"

She pushed her hair back from her forehead and I saw she wasn't yet out of her twenties, but her prettiness had already been worn away. "I knows him."

The child's face pressed to the screen. "What's he saying about my daddy?"

"Jurlean, get your butt away from here or I'm gonna have to whup you and I ain't lying about that."

Chris said, "So you know LeCharles—and Ellis Lee?"

"You heard my little girl," said the woman with a proud thrust of her chin. "You talking about her daddy."

I stepped toward her. "Ellis Lee is your husband?"

"Not hardly. We never married, but we got Jurlean and we live together—up until they took him away. Now I be living with his brother and them." She looked out past the rental car. I couldn't see anything in her face except reluctance to go on talking to us.

"Tell me, what—"

Chris interrupted me. "Where is everybody?"

"You mean LeCharles and them? His kids is all in school. Him and Sandra is at work." She turned and peered back into the kitchen. "Pretty quick I gots to go to work too."

Chris removed a pack of cigarettes from his shirt pocket and offered her one. She shook her head. "What's your name?"

"Tamara Delilah Redwing."

"Redwing, huh?" Chris's eyes followed an island of smoke as it coasted away. "Sounds like you might be American Indian."

"Might be," she said.

He nodded, looking at the ground. "Have you got time to talk about Ellis Lee? Later, maybe?"

Her eyes flicked away. "What you want to know about him?"

"We might be able to help with his case. But we need information."

"His case?" She laughed harshly. "Ellis ain't got no case. Y'all just wasting your time." She turned around and called into the house. "Jurlean, go on and fetch your shoes now. Ain't going down there looking like no naked toe hayseed today, girl!"

I couldn't take another second of this. "What did he do, Tamara? Would you tell me that? Please!"

The woman who had borne his child, who had lived with him until "they took him away," assessed me coldly. "Y'all don't know?" She gazed upward where a boulevard of clouds bisected an innocent blue sky. When she brought her eyes back to me, they were narrow. "What you be wanting with him?"

"I met him at Parchman. Well, I mean—" I was flustered. "I talked to him, I didn't meet him."

"You was at the Farm? You?"

"I was a Freedom Rider."

"Yeah?" She turned back to the house. "Jurlean, get your rump out here now. I ain't going to be late serving that lunch and you sit up here talking about you ain't got no good shoes to wear." She smoothed the front of her dress and patted her hair, as if we'd already gone and she was standing there alone. But then looked at me again. "If you talked to him, why'n't you ask him your own self what he done?"

"I did."

The screen door opened and Jurlean came out, barefoot.

"You better get them shoes on, girl!"

Eyes darker than her mother's, the child slyly withdrew a pair of worn sandals from behind her back, but her mother had already turned away. "I reckon if Ellis don't want to tell you, I ain't going to."

"Oh my god!"

Chris threw a warning glance at me and said, "We can't help him until we know what he was convicted of. At least give us the name of his lawyer, would you do that much?"

"I don't know no lawyer."

"Mama, this strap's broke."

"Just wear it loose. C'mon."

"Does he have a lawyer?"

The woman shrugged. "I don't know."

I went close to her and said, "You realize he will die if somebody doesn't help him."

Her eyes were bottomless. "Can't nobody help Ellis. He told me that the first day I knowed him." She looked across a field behind the house to where a row of naked trees fingered the sky. "C'mon, Jurlean."

"Can I give you a ride?" asked Chris.

A shadow of contempt crossed her face. "I don't believe I be getting into no car with y'all, thank you kindly."

Chris shot me an unspoken "I-told-you-so." I watched the woman's narrow back and squared shoulders as she moved away from us, down the driveway. She was near the end of it when I yelled, "Wait!" She hesitated, half-turning, Jurlean's hand clamped in her own. I jogged toward them, but she turned then and kept going. "Please wait. Just tell me one thing—that's all—just tell me when."

I hadn't noticed her eyebrows before. They were downy bits of black fluff. She drew them together. "When?" she said, as if I'd asked an interesting question and she wanted to ponder it. She peered down at her daughter's head, and I too looked down at the narrow threads of scalp between the braids. After several seconds, without looking up, Tamara spoke. I had to bend toward her to catch the words: "Be next

155

month. The eighteenth." I expected tears, I suppose, because when she lifted her head, I was surprised to see her eyes were dry. "The eighteenth it all be over."

I swallowed.

"I gots to go." She nodded, like someone passing me in church, and hurried down the road, walking with her child between tall rows of scabbed poplars. Everything in Mississippi, I thought, was sick, even the trees.

18

CHRIS SAID, "Now will you accept that it's hopeless?"

I shook my head, but suddenly I wasn't thinking about Ellis Lee. "What's that coming?"

"What's what?" Chris peered down the road, where dust was kicking up. "Shit, shit, shit."

A sheriff's car pulled into the driveway.

"How did they find us?"

"You did everything but send them a telegram, Jeri."

Two men in uniform opened their doors and, to my astonishment, crouched behind them, pointing their guns at us. My heart jackhammered and I swayed on my feet.

"Turn around and get down on your faces! Get them legs spread!"

Chris pulled me to the ground, shouting, "Okay, okay!"

"Spread your arms!"

I obeyed, panting. Dust rose up, clotting in my mouth. Gravel bit into my shins. A shadow fell across me. The toe of a boot prodded my rib cage. "What's your name, gal?"

I told him in a choked voice.

"What y'all doing on this here property?"

Chris said, "Visiting."

"Appears to me there ain't nobody around for y'all to visit. Appears to me y'all are guilty of breaking and entering these premises."

By craning my neck I could see the screen door stood ajar and Jurlean had not closed the kitchen door behind it.

"If anything's missing, y'all be in violation of section 27-18 of the penal code. Felony burglary."

"We didn't take anything," I said. "We haven't even been in that house."

"Is that right? Well, Robby, I think you better take a look. See can you confirm their story."

I don't know how long we lay on the ground. It seemed like hours but was probably only five or ten minutes while the deputy pretended to search the house. Chris's face was turned away, his arms and legs twitching. I wished I could touch him. I owed him such an apology. LeCharles was supposed to tell me Ellis Lee was innocent and I'd tell the lawyers in Chicago and they'd rush down here and save his life. And I'd be a hero. Just like in the movies. But I wasn't a hero. I was trouble.

From the house I heard a faint tinkling sound. Breaking glass.

"Hey, white boy," said the man I assumed was the sheriff. He bent toward Chris and grabbed a fistful of his hair. Chris's eyes rolled up. "What'cha doing breaking into some poor nigger house?"

Chris said nothing and the sheriff shoved his face back into the gravel. The deputy came back out. He walked on stilt legs, incredibly long, thin poles. The dirt settled over his boots as he scuffed toward us, and I winced as he stopped directly in front of me, one arrowhead toe aimed at my left eye. I lowered my face. He drawled, "Well, that place sure is a mess." The sheriff chuckled. "You never seen the likes of it. Every damn pillow's positively ripped apart, refrigerator door tore off—Jesus, and all them windows broke."

"We didn't—!"

The pointed toe struck me on the side of my cheek, sending waves of pain through my eye, into my teeth. I screamed and Chris scrambled to a crouch, which I couldn't see, but I heard. "Son of a bitch!" he yelled and then I heard his ribs snap, although I didn't understand what I was hearing until later.

When I could focus a little, I saw Chris lying on his side, clutching his armpit, his face twisted. The deputy said, "Every mattress in the place is wrecked."

The sheriff poked me. "Get up."

The handcuffs bit into my wrists. Beside me Chris looked bleak. Blood trickled from one corner of his mouth and his lips were raw. He was breathing tentatively. The sheriff shoved first me and then Chris—who whimpered—into the back seat of his cruiser.

"I am so sorry about this, Chris." He shook his head, looking pointedly toward the front seat. "I hope you don't hate me, but I wouldn't blame you if you did."

"Shut up back there," the sheriff said. "Robby, you take care of that car, you hear?" He swung around to Chris. "Your key in the ignition?" Chris nodded. "Bring it round the station, okay, Robby?"

"Will do."

"Oh, Jesus, Chris," I whispered, "what're we going to do?"

"It's what *they're* going to do that worries me."

The deputy, his small mouth comical as the slit at the end of a penis, gave us a happy grin. "You got it, boy," he said in the rolling pitch of a game show MC.

19

A DARK HAND twisted in through my bars, fingers wiggling. "C'mon, white girl. Gimme some smokes. Pony up."

I eased away from that side of my cell. "I don't smoke."

The hand went limp, but then the fingers patted the wall and turned over. The cupped palm looked coy. "C'mon, baby, don't be a tight-ass."

"I swear. I don't smoke."

Again the hand sagged, but this time its owner resigned herself to defeat. She withdrew it. "My name's Wanda. What's yours, white girl?"

"I'm not white."

"You means you wishes you wasn't white. And I expects, from the way you talk, you better off colored in here. These honkies don't take no shine to peoples talk like y'all."

Wisps of smoke drifted from her cell. "You have a cigarette!"

"Less'n a pack," she said, sounding offended. "What you

in for?"

I lay down on my bunk. "Stupidity."

"We most of us be in here for that. I bet I knows. You one of them civil righters."

"What's that sound?" I shot to my feet. "Is that a shower?"

"They getting ready to clean us up."

I steadied myself against the bars. "Are they going to beat us?"

"Girl, if they didn't beat you already, they ain't gonna."

"But what's that smell?"

"Bug poison. Give you a stomachache. One girl got pemonia after they pour that mess all over her. Try not to breathe is the best way."

I began to sob.

"Hey, c'mon, now, baby." Wanda's hand slipped back into my cell. "Hold onto this. You be all right." Her fingers wrapped around mine. "Ain't nothing to be scared of. Just a little shower. Now tell me your name, honey."

I croaked, "Jeri."

"Welcome to Marivale Workhouse, Jeri. You going to see, peoples in here, we looks out for each other. You be okay."

I sniffed and wiped my face with the back of my hand. "So what're you in here for?"

"A long time," she chuckled, taking back her hand. More smoke drifted out of her cell. "I cut my old man."

"You what?"

"I be trying to dust his broom but that man ain't having none of it."

I had no idea what she meant. "But is he going to be all right?"

Someone was walking toward our cells. I heard Wanda exhale and then the soft shush of her foot grinding out her cigarette. "I hope to hell he ain't," she said as her cell door opened.

* * *

"This here's where you sleep." The matron, pale and bony—a different breed from Mrs. Buckerfield at Parchman—pointed to a narrow cot and slammed out of the prison dormitory. I wondered if the gray sheet was safe to lie on.

A woman with hair that stuck up like a black hedge said, "Hey" from the bunk next to mine. "I'm Dixie Dinah. And that on the other side of you's Mary. She ain't right in the head so don't pay her no never mind."

Mary looked about fifteen or sixteen. She lay on her bunk staring at the ceiling, her hands folded over her massive belly.

Dixie Dinah said, "What you doing in here with us, white girl?"

A gaunt woman on the other side of Dixie Dinah called out, "Hey, Jeri. It's me, Wanda."

I recognized her voice. "Wanda. With the cigarettes," I said. "Thanks for holding my hand."

"She one of them civil righters," Wanda told Dixie Dinah. "She all right."

"You in here for the demonstrating?"

"Trespass. And you?"

"Oh, you know." Dixie Dinah rolled her eyes. "I has a customer who sometime don't like to pay me. He call the sheriff and here I be."

On the floor, a radio rattled with static and the voice of an on-air preacher. I looked down the two long rows of bunks. There were about twenty women in the cell. Most of them showed no interest in me.

"You be working in the kitchen with Maxine come

tomorrow," said Dixie Dinah. "Wanda always work the laundry—"

I lifted an eyebrow at Wanda. "Honey, once these folks starts putting you in the jailhouse, they be like a cat get used to peeing on your bed. See you in the street, they has to take you in. It don't matter what for. Sometimes it be the drunk. Sometimes it be the vacancy. This time it happen I cut Willie, cut him good, thank Jesus."

Dixie Dinah shook her head. "Like I was saying, Jeri, Maxine done lost her last girl yesterday so I pretty sure you be going with her to the kitchen."

I smiled at an old woman with purple splotches under her eyes, leaning over her knees, smoking. She grunted but she didn't return my smile.

"Don't mind her. Maxine don't like nobody."

The lights and the radio went off. "They cuts the 'lectricity at ten," said Dixie Dinah in the dark. "The bathroom to your left. You need a match, honey, just take the book from the floor. Now goodnight, white girl."

From Mary's bed, I heard the squishy sounds of her fingers moving in and out between her legs. Every minute or two, she gasped. I rolled over, toward Dixie Dinah's bunk. "Best get used to it," she murmured to me. "It be going on all night long, every night."

Mary did keep at it throughout the night. It bothered me a lot more than the women banging in and out of the bathroom, but it wasn't noise or even Mary's masturbating keeping me awake. T.J. didn't know where I was and I kept thinking maybe she'd had another heart attack when she didn't hear from me.

And, like a nagging line from some song, I told myself over and over that when my thirty days in the workhouse were up, Ellis Lee would have only ten more to live.

* * *

163

Wanda's shift had crept up around her thighs, exposing a grey tuft of pubic hair. A jar lid rested on her navel, her cigarette burned almost to her knuckles. She'd just spent the better part of our one free hour hunched over her toes, squeezing out streams of green pus.

"How you like working the kitchen?"

"It's all right. But Maxine doesn't talk to me."

"Good. You see your man?"

"No, I didn't see him all day. Did anybody tell you his work assignment?"

She shook her head. "But I keep asking around for you."

"He has to be here. They brought him down with me."

"Then somebody know where he is. Ain't no secrets in here." I was startled by tears swarming into my eyes, the memory of Ellis Lee's warm voice heavy on my heart. Wanda looked at me sharply. "Girl, what make you turn on the water like that?"

I blew my nose and told her. Wanda stopped with a fresh cigarette halfway to her mouth. "Say what? How you know somebody on the death row?"

She was amused by my description of kneeling over my toilet and talking into the vent but she did a double-take when I said Ellis Lee's name.

"Naw. Really? He on the row?"

"You know him?"

"Used to know his kin. Didn't know 'bout him being on the row."

"What do you know about him?"

"Ellis put away for armed robbery—I think that be about two year ago, maybe a little more. I did hear he 'scaped." She looked at me closely. "You not sweet on him?"

"No. It's not that. He sounded like a nice man."

"Ellis Lee?" She cackled.

"He was nice to me," I said. "I better get ready for bed."

"Hold on. I know Ellis Lee's peoples but him I really didn't know except to say *how do*. I hear things, and some of them wasn't too good. But some peoples did say he bighearted. He love his baby, everybody say that."

I squeezed her hand. It was little enough she gave me, but more than anyone else had to say for him.

* * *

Wanda said the sisters from Alabama were arrested driving a station wagon loaded down with twenty cases of white lightning, visible on the straight Mississippi highway for practically a mile because the rear bumper barely cleared the road. Outside of playing cards with Maxine some nights, neither had much to say, not even to each other. Even so, they both took some of Mary's work in the laundry to keep her from being thrown into solitary.

"I does the rest," Wanda said. "Afore me, there was another gal used to watch out for Mary. I tole you we takes care."

On a cot across from Mary's, a woman with a scarred face and hair like soiled suds kept scraping a spoon up and down the cement wall.

I whispered, "Why is she doing that?"

"Fixing to cut Mary, if we lets her. But I cut Vivian myself afore I see that sick child sliced. First she put some goofy dust on Mary pillow but when that don't work, Vivian start in with that knife. She crazy, in the workhouse for fifteen years cause she set fire to her sister bed. Vivian say onliest thing she sorry about is her man come in the room and roll that gal up in the blanket. Turn out, Vivian man be her sister's back door man."

Vivian, making sweeping arcs with the spoon, looked like someone acting out a primitive religious ceremony. She spat and a wad of thick saliva crossed the space between her bunk and Mary's, landing on the girl's leg. If Mary noticed, she didn't show it. She made no move to wipe it off, just kept staring up at the ceiling.

* * *

Dixie Dinah told me at breakfast why Vivian wanted to stab Mary.

"Vivian particular about her food."

"In here?"

Dixie Dinah shrugged. "She like it clean. But Mary unsteady on her feets. Just afore y'all come, she fall in Vivian beans. Stuck her hand in there. And you know where that hand be all the time. Vivian, she make a grab for Mary's tray but Mary hold on tight. Never saw that gal move so quick. She like her dinner. They tugging back and forth and that plate go flying. Them guards make Vivian eat that slop off the floor. She like to die."

I looked at the gray lump of grits on my plate. "So how'd Mary wind up in here?"

"Poor Mary. She dry so long." Dixie Dinah shook her head. I was getting accustomed to hearing things I didn't understand. "She take money out of a lady's chifforobe. Mary clean that lady house for a month but the lady refuse to pay her. Mary figure she owed ten dollars, she take ten dollars. They was more in the drawer but Mary only took what was coming to her." Dixie Dinah pushed her plate away and stood up. "Ain't no way a nigger can get away with that in Mississippi."

* * *

We were washing dishes and Maxine told me she was

sixty-eight years old and had spent thirty-four years in jail. Half her life. I thought about my grandmother who wasn't that old and who was probably cursing me because she was paying for a telephone in her hospital room that never rang. I'd asked about getting a letter out to T.J. Wanda just laughed. "Girl, you gots to be dreaming."

"I had heat stroke," Maxine told me, as if I'd asked her a question. "That's all it was." After that she confined herself to nodding like one of those toy gooney birds that keep dipping their beaks in a glass of water. All the while, her fingers kept plucking clean hot glasses from the jaws of the steamer.

Wanda told me Maxine had gone into Cock of the Walk in Williamton and ordered a glass of iced tea. "Hadn't been for you freedomers, probably them folks wouldn't of done nothing 'cept send a crazy old nigger home. I expect they was hoping to keep y'all out of Williamton by giving Maxine six months."

20

EVERY DAY I looked for Chris in the dining hall where we had just fifteen minutes to wolf down slimy greens and gray sausage. Dry cheese-food sandwiches. The biscuits kept me going. Somehow the cook never wrecked the biscuits.

Whenever I passed the laundry to lug another load of dishes back over to the Marivale County Home for the Aged, I squinted through the steam at the workers, looking for Chris. Wanda told me he wasn't in there but I was like someone who's lost something and keeps going back to the same drawer, positive it has to be in there.

Dixie Dinah gave baths to the old people in the County Home behind the jail. She'd promised to keep an eye out for Chris but whenever I saw her, she just shook her head. On the way back to the kitchen, I'd scan the faces of the men in striped pants jockeying carts of folded sheets and towels, or going the other way, hauling drawstring bags of linen so foul smelling, I thought I'd vomit whenever a trolley rolled past. If I spotted white skin, I'd check under the brim of the baseball cap the men had to wear, my breath hitching in my throat if the hair was butter-yellow. But the face was never Chris's face.

At night, I tossed on my cot, aching for cold water and fresh air. And every second, chugging away in the back of my mind, T.J. was pinned to her bed and Ellis Lee was trapped in his cell. And panic flooded my body because I had no idea where they had taken Chris or what they had done to him. And all of it was my fault.

* * *

During the hour between work and lights out, Maxine folded and unfolded an old letter from her son in Chicago. Dixie Dinah told me she liked to look at the swirls of his handwriting. She couldn't read but she knew the letter by heart. Some nights she dictated a response to Vivian, who would take a break from working on her knife to write down every word—which was pointless. As Wanda said, you couldn't get a letter out. But Vivian's kindness softened my attitude toward her. When the lights went out and Mary began rubbing herself and moaning, I felt some compassion for Vivian's urge to get even.

* * *

The window flashed yellow and from across the fields to the highway I heard the running water sound of cars passing below us. Some of the prisoners were assigned to the farm and in the daytime, through the narrow kitchen window, I had watched their stooped bodies working in the hot sun. The kitchen and laundry workers said it was the hardest job. The farm workers slept in barracks in the foothills. Was Chris out there? If he was, I would've seen him in the dining hall anyway. Wanda swore he wasn't with that crew.

Vivian's spoon-knife kept grinding. "Will you fight her if

she goes after Mary?"

Wanda said, "How about you fighting her, Miss Geraldine?"

"I'd be too scared."

"You be surprised, girl. Truth ain't hardly in what peoples think they is." She put out the bit of cigarette she'd smoked and lowered the jar lid toward the floor. Mid-way down, the lid fell out of her hand. She looked at the strewn ashes and butts and fell back against her pillow. Across the way, Vivian was checking the sharpness of the spoon handle against her thumb pad. "I expect time coming somebody have to fight her."

* * *

Vivian stood at the foot of my cot. Even though the electricity had been cut off, I could see her face clearly. She was the color of the pus seeping out of Wanda's toes. She held a huge garish pink Bible out as if she were offering it to me. I had to have it, but every time I reached for it, she drew it back, her lips twisting open to expose metal teeth.

Vivian turned into Dorothy who began tearing out pages, wadding them up, and shoving them into her mouth. She was chewing up the Bible. I flung myself at her, a move I knew was suicidal.

"Girl, you having a bad dream." I woke to find someone on the cot with me. My breath was coming in gusts, my arms and legs felt like running water. "You all right, Jeri? It's me, okay?" Dixie Dinah held me until my body relaxed. "You lay back down here, baby. You be okay."

"Eight days," I wept. "Eight days."

"Well, girl, you gots a lot more to go. Best not to count them."

"I can't—I'm falling apart. Chris is somewhere, I

don't know where. And I'm the one who put him in here," I sobbed.

"Hey, didn't no one put him in here except the police, and you remember that."

"It's not true." I writhed on my cot. "I did it. I screwed everything up. My grandmother's really sick and she doesn't even know I'm in here."

"Well, we can fix that anyways. You can writes to your granny."

"How? We can't get mail out."

Dixie Dinah stroked my hair. "I get you a letter out. I steal you a stamp and some paper from one of them old peoples. Get you a envelope. Those old peoples always be forgetting what's in they rooms. Leave it to me."

"Oh, Dixie, thank you." I hugged her.

She patted my check and went back to her cot. "You go on to sleep now, hear?"

I lay there for several minutes, listening to the evenness of Dixie Dinah's breath as she slipped back into her own dreams, clearly more peaceful than mine. Every time I closed my eyes, I saw Chris, holding his side, biting down hard to keep from crying out. His eyes scalded me with accusations. I had sacrificed him to save a man no one else thought deserved to be saved.

* * *

Over breakfast the next morning, I saw him, looking a good deal thinner. I got up and hissed, "Chris! Over here!" Wanda pulled me back into my seat just before the guard turned around. It was agony to be close to him and not speak. I was so relieved to see he wasn't seriously hurt. When we lined up to go back to work, I mouthed, "Where are you working?"

He didn't answer. I moved closer to him and murmured,

"Where are you—?"

"Girl!" Wanda grabbed me. "You wants to get him put in the hole?"

"I know, but—"

"But ain't nothing. Let him be."

* * *

True to her word, Dixie Dinah brought me some paper and an envelope. "Tomorrow I put your letter with the mail go out. And here's an old magazine I found over there. You can use that to hold the paper when you write."

I thanked her but my mind wasn't on the letter. I was waiting for Wanda to come back and tell me if Chris worked in the laundry, if he'd said anything to her about me. But Wanda didn't come back to the dormitory after dinner.

Vivian was working on her knife. "Where's Wanda?" I asked her.

Her reddened eyes looked through me. "How should I know?"

"She with the warden," said Dixie Dinah.

"Is she in trouble?"

"Naw. This be her week."

"When I went," said Maxine, "his wife serve patty. That's what she call it. Look like something already been eat. I had to carry it around on a tray and ask everybody did they want some patty. I don't believe any of them knowed what it was. We had to throw it all out when we cleaned up."

"When I had to serve," said Dixie Dinah, "the warden stuck his hand up under my dress and his wife come in and seen him."

"You lying," said one of the bootleggers, but she looked interested.

"I am lying," grinned Dixie Dinah. "About his wife coming in." She stood up and went into the bathroom.

I was staring out the window, which I did most nights. Whenever I looked down at the snaking highway, I thought about the people passing this workhouse on that road, not glancing up, not thinking about who was locked up behind these walls. It gave me an odd sensation. Those people were a few hundred yards away and yet they were in some other universe.

"I about to cut you, bitch," said Vivian. I turned from the window. The spoon knife glittered in Vivian's hand. "Time's up." She started toward Mary's bunk. The mountain of flesh stretched out on the cot didn't flinch.

"Don't start none, won't be none," said one of the bootleggers. "She ain't messing with you, Vivian."

"She always be messing with me with them little voodoo eyes she gots."

"You crazy, girl."

"Don't be calling me crazy. I like to cut that shit-eating grin off your damned face when I gets through with this cunt. I seen you, nigger," she said to Mary, who still didn't move.

"Don't make out like you ain't heard me, nigger. Always playing the fool. Looky here, bitch. You feel this knife, you come awake in a hurry. You listen to me, nigger, you set me up. You done that to me on purpose and you better believe I knows it."

My eyes found a small inscription on the rail at the foot of my cot: EAT ME. Cautiously, I set the magazine and the piece of paper I'd been writing on down on the floor. I'd only gotten as far as "Dear T.J." anyway. I felt odd, weirdly disconnected. I almost giggled, as I'd done at the train depot when Ned lay, curled up on the ground, ready to receive his punishment.

"What you want with that baby?" demanded Dixie

Dinah, coming out of the bathroom. "Onliest thing she know is playing with her own pussy. She don't be thinking about you, girl. Just leave her be."

"Mary, Mary, so contrary," crooned Vivian, "I is coming to cut your ass."

"I say leave that child alone, Vivian," snapped Dixie Dinah. "Or do I have to go upside your nappy head?"

"You be getting yours after I cut this black cunt."

Dixie Dinah took off one shoe. It was a pitiful weapon with a tiny round hole, like a cigarette burn, in the sole. But her face burned with an incandescence that might've started with syphilis, which Wanda said it did, but now looked like the outdoorsy glow of good health. She looked radiant as she advanced with her silly shoe.

My fingers circled the bed railing, covering the letters EAT ME. I was riveted by a premonition of what it would look like if Vivian stabbed Dixie Dinah. I saw the sticky red blood, the corpse, the creepy lifelike expression on her face. I knew I couldn't bear it if Vivian hurt her. Dixie Dinah was worth a hundred Vivians.

"Don't do that."

Vivian cocked one jagged eyebrow at me. "Say what?"

I said thickly, "She's dead."

Vivian's face crumpled in disbelief. "What you talking about, white nigger?"

I looked into her crazed eyes and said again, "Mary's dead."

Vivian glanced down at the placid face on the pillow. Mary didn't move. Her eyelids didn't flicker. "Shit, you pure crazy."

"She is." I felt the presence of the women behind me as if they were an onrushing tide, pushing me forward. Someone snickered and Dixie Dinah said, "Shush!" and the room fell again into a sickly quaking silence. Vivian gaped at me, wary. "Mary was already dead when I got here."

Vivian spat on the floor. "Girl, you a liar and the truth ain't in you. Expect me to believe that shit? She been up and moving around, ain't you seen that?"

"Believe whatever you want." I thought of the sharpened blade, of its warped bowl snug in the palm of Vivian's hand. I wondered how it would feel to be stabbed. But Vivian didn't move toward me. "You stick her with that knife and you've got a very nasty surprise coming." I pinched my nostrils. "She stinks. She's been rotting away. Pieces of her skin are going to come off and stick to you. Her flesh is like soup already."

Vivian took a step backward. I hooded the elation in my eyes, pretending to be intent on inspecting my fingers, working a piece of dirt out of my thumbnail.

"What you talking about? You cracking up, girl. Talking about people's rotten—ugh!"

My forced grin felt as if it might jerk off my face, but I made myself lean toward her. "Go ahead," I urged. "Cut her. Stick it in her. I dare you. I want to see it. I want to see her insides explode in your face. That's what happens, you know. Somebody like that—her guts will bust out and get all over you. You can't wash that stink off, you can't. It'll be there for months. Ask any doctor."

Behind me the cell door opened. I hoped it was the matron, but when the dormitory stayed quiet, I knew Wanda must've come in.

Vivian had not moved. Her eyes were anchored in mine. I got off the cot and walked toward her. "Come on, Vivian. What're you scared of? Go ahead and stick her. I want to see it. She's a swamp now. You'll probably be sucked in. Nothing will be left of you that isn't covered in slime." I inched closer, reaching my arm out as if to shove her toward Mary. "Hurry up. What're you waiting for?"

"You insane, girl. Just get on away from me. Don't you try and touch me, hear?" She threw out her hand, as if to ward me off, and stumbled back to her cot. She put the spoon-knife under her pillow and sat down on her bed to remove her shoes, never taking her eyes from my face. I backed carefully onto my own bed. I held my breath so as not to shatter the brittle threads holding us all right where we were.

* * *

Dear T.J.,

I'm so sorry I'm not there with you. I wanted to be and I thought I would by now. I think about you all the time. I love you so much—please get better. Before I could start home, I got arrested again and I'm in the workhouse in Marivale County, Mississippi, for thirty days. Don't worry. I'm okay, just worried sick about you.

I'll be home as soon as I can after I get out. I hope Rita's still there with you and she's staying sane. See you soon.

Lots of love, Jeri

21

MARY DIDN'T get out of her bunk the next morning. She lay breathing through her mouth, one hand resting between her legs, the other wedged between her teeth. Wanda and Dixie Dinah tried to drag her out of bed but she was too heavy. They had to give up. When we lined up to go down to breakfast, the matron came in and looked at her. "Get up," she said, poking her arm, but Mary didn't move.

I asked Wanda what would happen to Mary. "They be taking her over to the county home. It be a damned shame too. Colored people at the county home, some of them lives in they own shit. Somebody like Mary, they don't never clean her up. The only ones get paid attention be the white folks. Nobody give a damn about old colored peoples, not even the niggers supposed to take care of them. And peoples like Mary never will get out of that place."

I pictured an inmate, her feet propped on a chair while next to her an old Negro lady faded like a dying picture tube into a shadow on the bed. It was Mary fifty years from now.

Fifteen and headed to the county home forever.

* * *

Wanda said, "Roxanne told me she have a sister lives over to Barrieville, outside of Colfax."

Roxanne slept at the other end of the dormitory and she worked with Wanda in the laundry. "Yes?"

"She say to tell you there was a white man stayed over to her sister's place."

"And? And?"

"Hold onto your pants, girl. Roxanne say the only reason she remember was it be a Wednesday and Roxanne and her sister supposed to be going down to Jackson to visit they Mama, and her sister say she can't do it, this man be giving her too much money. He give her fifty bucks."

"C'mon, Wanda," I pleaded. "Does this have anything to do with Ellis Lee or not?"

"Might be. You has to decide for your own self. Thing is, it stayed with Roxanne all this time on account of that Wednesday was the only one they ever missed spending with they Mama, and on account it was so much money. Her sister say the sheriff come out to the house and ask why that man come around bothering honest colored folks. Something about how that man come to some colored man's job, asking a lot of questions. Roxanne can't really recall. Sheriff say for that man to go on home."

"What about Ellis Lee? Does Roxanne think the man might've been a reporter was doing a story on him?"

"Roxanne only know a white man be staying at her sister's house, paying fifty dollars. That's it."

"Okay, give me the sister's name. When I get out I'll go ask her about it."

"You crazy as Vivian think you are. Don't you remember

what you told me the sheriff done to those peoples' house in Colfax? You think Roxanne want her sister's house looking like that?"

She was right, of course. It was a dumb idea. "But, Wanda," I whined, "what good it does me to know that some man from some place went to Colfax to look into something at some time?"

"She ain't sure 'bout the time. She say it be a year back, or maybe two or three, but she do remember where that man from. Roxanne say another reason it stay with her is that man say he come from New Orleans. Roxanne love New Orleans. She ain't never been there. She just love to hear about it."

A white man looking for a black man in Colfax didn't necessarily have anything to do with Ellis Lee, but something in me said it did. I felt sure it did.

* * *

On the twelfth morning a guard took me from the kitchen to the warden's office. "Come in, gal. Come on in."

After the cement walls of the workhouse dormitory, the relative opulence of the warden's office startled me. Van Gogh's Potato Eaters—I remembered it from a high school art class—hung behind the man at the desk. In his blue suit and neatly trimmed hair, the warden looked like a bank clerk.

He peered at me through wire-rimmed spectacles. I recognized the sheriff, who sat to one side of the office, in a cushioned chair, his boot aimlessly stabbing the air. Was he reminding me of the damage that boot could do? "Come on in," drawled the warden. "Y'all know each other, I expect."

He didn't suggest that I sit down and, anyway, there was no chair for me to sit in.

"C'mon, c'mon in here," he said. "We have a proposal."
I hung back. "What proposal?"

"Will you get in here? I don't like to shout." I moved closer to his desk. He leaned back and chewed on a cellophane wrapped cigar, saying, "I heard about that little altercation y'all had the other night."

I said, "What do you want?"

"I expect you be willing to leave this state soon as you released. Ain't no reason for y'all to be here in the first place, way I look at it."

"What're you saying? I can go?"

"Under certain conditions."

"And Chris—he can leave too?"

"Of course. The young man's already agreed. The only question remaining is whether you will accompany him."

"Why are you so hot for us to leave?"

The warden shrugged. Beside him the sheriff stabbed at his teeth with a toothpick. "I believe we been more patient with y'all than the situation calls for. I wonder how long the people of California would stand for it if we Mississippians climbed on buses and started overrunning your state, breaking your laws, telling y'all how to live." His eyes glittered. "Now, Miss Turner," he continued, saying my name as if he wished to rid his mouth of it as quickly as possible, "I am agreeable to commuting your sentence if I have your word that you will get out of Mississippi today and keep out."

Cut off from Ellis Lee. "Do you know what Ellis Lee's on death row for?"

"Who?"

But the sheriff sat forward. "Ellis Lee ain't none of your business, young lady. That boy was convicted in a court of law. His own people ain't trying to get him out and for good reason."

If I agreed to leave, I didn't have to keep my word. I remembered that much from working in the basement at

McCullough Worthington. A contract made under duress wasn't binding in court. I snorted then, thinking, *Right. If they arrest me again, I'll sue them.*

"Well, Miss Turner? Do we have your word?"

"You'll commute my sentence? A warden can do that?"

"The governor will take my recommendation."

"If I called Mr. Barnett after he took your *recommendation*, what do you want'a bet he'd say, 'Geraldine *who*?' I know what you guys are up to. You're going to collect money for two prisoners who aren't in your jail. I wonder how mu—" I broke off as it dawned on me I must be as wacky as my mother. "Okay, but how do I know you guys won't arrest me for escaping the minute I go out?"

"And just why would we do that?" The sheriff was inspecting a gob of something speared on his toothpick. "I think you've been watching too many Hollywood movies."

"We want the same thing, Miss Turner. You want to go and I want you to go. All you got to keep in mind is there'll be hell to pay if y'all stay round here."

"The only question being," I said, remembering the destruction of LeCharles's house, "who would pay."

The sheriff wore a satisfied smirk. "And that's something y'all don't understand. The colored people in this state don't want you here. The white people don't want you. Nobody wants you. Y'all do nothing but bring trouble to everybody."

Behind and above the warden, the Potato Eaters were intent on their meal, their peasant ugliness a matter of indifference except to outside eyes. "Get going. The matron will bring you your things."

"And Chris?"

"Just step into the other room."

But I wavered. It could be a trick. Chris had been hidden away before. "I have to be sure you're letting him out too."

The warden was unpeeling the cellophane from his cigar. His eyes lifted to mine. They were the color of razor blades. "Would I lie to you?"

"Yes."

There was a long pause in which the sheriff shifted in his chair. I made no move toward the door.

"Never mind. He's out there."

"Prove it."

"You goddamned bitch! If you don't—" The warden half-rose from his chair, but the sheriff waved a hand.

"Go on," he said, pointing toward the window. "Look outside."

I saw a blue station wagon beyond the gate. Two people stood beside it. They were too far away for me to make out who they were except to see they were black. But a blonde man came out of the building and moved toward the car. I recognized his walk.

"Okay," I said with a broad smile. "But can I say goodbye to Dixie Dinah and Wanda?"

"You cannot. Now get out of my workhouse."

* * *

A guard nodded from the open doorway of a booth. The gate slid open. I stepped through it and couldn't restrain the impulse to spread my arms and whirl around under the pastel sky. Even in a heat as dense as custard, I did a little jig before I walked toward the station wagon. In the front seat were Reverend Carroll and Sweet Pea.

Chris clambered out of the back. I hugged him tentatively. "How're your ribs?"

"Not as bad as they were a week ago. For at least the last ten minutes I've been sitting here wondering if they were going to let you out after all."

"I almost did talk them out of it."

He grinned. "I figured you were doing something along those lines. That's my Jeri."

Reverend Carroll called out, "Y'all best get in here. We need to get going."

"Hello, Reverend. Hello, Sweet Pea." I slid across the warm sticky seat. Reverend Carroll began backing the car away from the workhouse. "I don't know how you folks did this, but I'm sure grateful. How'd you know we were here?"

"Sweet Pea kept after me, saying you left your suitcase behind, Miss Geraldine. I figured y'all must be off doing some work for CORE. But yesterday I saw Paul and I asked him about y'all and he say y'all come up here on your own."

"But how'd you know we were in the workhouse?"

He grimaced into the rear view mirror. "There was only two places to look. In the workhouse or the graveyard."

Sweet Pea got onto her knees and grinned at us over the seat back. "Reverend Carroll told the sheriff if they didn't let y'all out, we be bringing two or three hundred Freedom Riders to Colfax. He knowed they ain't got jail enough to take care of that many pickets."

"Not to mention how sorely the funds from the county budget would be missed," Reverend Carroll said. "Now I'd be mighty appreciative if y'all would slide yourselves down back there. There's them as would be drawn to this car like bees to a picnic. And, Sweet Pea, you turn around and pretend you're a lady."

Chris and I scrunched on the floor. I saw him wince and his forehead beaded with sweat. "Do you have anything for the pain?" I asked him.

He nodded. "They took me to the infirmary as soon as I got here. The ribs are taped so I just have to wait it out and take my pain meds."

Reverend Carroll said, "Where's your car? Over to the jail in Colfax?"

"Should be," huffed Chris. "Sheriff told me they left the keys in the glove compartment. But drop us at the edge of town. I don't want them to have a chance to get back at you for the smart trick you pulled on them."

"Y'all would be in peril, if I did. Never mind about us. Those two or three hundred pretend Freedom Riders ought to keep the good old boys from messing with us."

As the car picked up speed on the highway, I whispered to Chris, "Where *were* you all that time? Were you in the infirmary?"

His face contorted, his breathing fast and shallow. "It's a long story."

"Jackson's a ways. We've got time."

"We're not going to Jackson."

I knew he was taking me to New Orleans and I knew that once we got there, CORE would fly me home. Between here and the airport, I had to put together a plan to keep myself off that plane.

"I looked everywhere for you. I kept pestering everyone, asking if they'd seen you."

His beautiful eyes hardened to dark blue glass. I suspected at that moment I stopped being *his Jeri*. But why? It was a reasonable question.

He shifted his shoulders, seeking a position that didn't jam the door handle or the window crank into him, and he propped himself to one side, away from the broken ribs, leaning his elbow on the car seat. I missed his first words. "… about your sparring match. And you were worried about *me* being dead?"

His curly yellow hair shone, strangely clean. "Did you guys get regular showers?"

His face squeezed shut like a fist. "Do you know how it made me feel when I heard about you and that lunatic?"

"Vivian? You know about that?"

"Was she coming after you? Because that's not what I heard."

"Come on, Chris. I couldn't stand there and watch her stab Dixie. Dixie was good to me."

"Another angelic felon? Another hapless victim? Are you planning to get Dixie a lawyer too?"

"Now that's not fair—"

"You talked me into this."

"I told you to let me come up here by myself."

"Right. You have to rescue everybody under the sun but I'm supposed to act like a coward and let a woman go off on a wild goose chase that could get her strung from a tree. And what was your plan, by the way? Were you going to walk around Colfax, yelling, 'LeCharles! LeCharles!'?"

"Stop making fun of me."

He held himself stiffly, trying in vain to protect his side from the bumping and swaying of the car. "You know what I think, Jeri? I think this Ellis Lee obsession is nothing more than you acting out your fantasy of a hero. Trouble is, your heroics cost me a lot more than I wanted to pay."

Sweet Pea twisted around in her seat. "Did y'all find out anything about that man? The one in the death cell?"

I asked Reverend Carroll if he had any tissue and he reached in the glove compartment and handed one back. I dabbed at my eyes.

"Did you?" repeated Sweet Pea.

"How do you know about him?"

Reverend Carroll yanked on the back of her shirt. "Sit down, young lady. I only agreed to let you come along after you promised to behave." To us, he said, "Would you believe it? This child threaten to run away from home—and threaten to do far worse too, less I bring her along. She scared her Mama so, that poor lady beg me to take Sweet Pea, even knowing it might prove dangerous. You a most shameful gal, Sweet Pea."

"I is behaving, Reverend Carroll. Look. I just turn my head a little bit." She tipped her head over the seat and rolled her eyes toward us on the floor. "I knows you trying to find out about that condemn man 'cause I asked the other girl stay with us."

"Thomasine?"

"She say you nuts."

"What Sweet Pea giveth," said Reverend Carroll, "she also taketh away."

Sweet Pea turned around at last and Chris and I fell into silence. Every minute or so, he writhed and occasionally he let out a muffled moan, but otherwise we sat, knee to knee, listening only to the occasional whoosh of a passing car. I wanted to tell him how sorry I was to have gotten him in such trouble but I couldn't get his accusation out of my mind. It was too close to what I'd wondered about myself a time or two.

At last we heard the splatter of gravel kicking up from under the tires.

Chris and I un-wedged ourselves and crawled out. We stood behind the jail in Colfax. Reverend Carroll had pulled up next to the rented Chevy. I glanced at the jail windows but I couldn't see anyone looking out at us.

Chris said, "I was afraid they might've wrecked it."

Reverend Carroll said, "Your suitcases are in the trunk."

"I'll get them," I said. "I don't think you should be lifting anything, Chris."

He shrugged and opened the door of the rental car.

Reverend Carroll said, "Well, all right then. I don't suppose y'all be coming back to Jackson?"

"No, sir," said Chris. "We're going right to New Orleans."

"Reverend Carroll," I said, bending down, "you've done so much, I hate to ask you for anything more. But it's not for me. I'm wondering, do you think you could find out what I've been trying to find out? I can't get Ellis Lee a lawyer until I know what he did."

Sweet Pea said, "You surely could do that, Reverend Carroll."

Looking straight ahead, he gripped his steering wheel. "Miss Geraldine, please don't take this amiss, but I have a message for you from Mr. Pelton. His secretary told him about your telephone call when he was up in New York and he consulted the CORE leadership there. Miss Geraldine, what they want is what these here folks want." He waved toward the jail. "They want that you should go on back home." He smiled apologetically. "I know that's hard for you to accept and I don't rightly blame you. But I can't go against CORE."

I stepped back. "Well, thanks anyway, Reverend Carroll. This was a brave thing to do and we appreciate it. And, Sweet Pea," I said, "I owe you, I really do. You're terrific."

"I can do it!" she said, throwing herself across Reverend Carroll to speak to me. "I can find out."

I knew with cold certainty exactly how Sweet Pea would go about trying to find out. "Don't you do that," I warned her. "I mean it. I know what you're thinking and I don't want you to do that."

She pretended to pout but she had to be relieved.

"I want to see is that car running all right," Reverend Carroll told Chris. "Then I believe we be on our way."

When the station wagon was gone and Chris had turned

the Chevy onto the highway, I said, "Now will you tell me?"

He pulled a pack of cigarettes from his shirt pocket and lit one. Blowing smoke through his teeth, he shook his head.

"Jeri, for once in your life, take no for an answer."

22

HE WOKE ME from a doze. "We're almost there."

I stretched and looked out the window at heat waves coming off the tar. "You can let me out when we get downtown."

"Uh uh. I'm taking you to the airport."

"But what about you, Chris? Aren't you going back to L.A.?"

He punched the lighter in. "I've been thinking about it and I decided I'm going to stay in New Orleans for a while. I want to work with CORE."

"But don't we have to get my plane ticket from the office?"

"I'll buy your ticket. CORE will reimburse me."

I didn't say anything but I felt his eyes on me.

"You're awfully quiet, Jer."

"I'm just thinking."

"About what?"

"Going home."

He pulled a thread of tobacco from the tip of his tongue. "I expected more of a fight."

"The last thing Mr. Starkweather said to me was there was no shame in giving up on a lost cause. And, like you said in the car—I don't have a right to put other people in danger for somebody like him."

"So you've decided he's a lost cause."

"That's what I said."

"And that's why you asked Reverend Carroll to find out what Ellis Lee did?"

"Well, I just thought—"

"And that's why you asked me if I could drop you downtown? Because he's a lost cause?"

"I thought CORE could take care of getting me to the airport. Aren't they downtown?"

He tossed his cigarette out the window. "Yeah, right."

"You don't need to come in," I told him when we approached the terminal. "Just give me the plane fare."

"We don't even know the flight schedule. There might not be a plane out of here until tomorrow."

"I don't mind camping here if I have to. It probably won't be more than a few hours. It's a big airport."

He turned into the lot and parked the car. "I know what you're up to, Jeri. I'm not stupid. You haven't given up at all. I want to know what you're planning."

"I'm not planning anything. You hate me now so I thought you'd be in a hurry to get rid of me."

His face softened. "Cut it out. You know I don't hate you."

"No? It sure sounded like it to me." I looked through the window. People lugging suitcases were moving in all directions. "I need to call my grandmother."

"You can call her inside," he said, opening his door.

"Okay," I said. "You were right. I'm not getting on any plane today." He closed his door and glared steadily through the windshield. "Look, you decided to stay here. Why can't I?"

"Because you're not staying to work with CORE."

"If my grandmother's okay, I will stay and work with them. I just have to look for something first."

"And what's that?"

"Some reporter from New Orleans wrote a story about Ellis Lee."

"Where did you hear that?"

"In the workhouse. He stayed with the sister of one of the inmates. He paid her fifty dollars. Nobody pays fifty dollars to stay in Colfax. That reporter went there to talk to Ellis Lee's brother, I know it. And it must've been around the time Ellis was sentenced to die."

"She said he was a reporter?"

"Why else would he be looking for Ellis Lee's brother?"

"Did she say he was looking for Ellis Lee's brother?"

I rolled my eyes. "What're you? The district attorney? This is my last chance, don't you see that?"

"Jeri, this sounds like pure speculation."

"Well, Chris, speculation's what I have left. And I'm not giving up as long as there's something I can do. You can dump me out here and I'll walk back to New Orleans if I have to. If you give me a ticket, I'll cash it in and live on it. If you don't, I don't care. I'll make my way somehow."

Twenty minutes later we stopped where William Blanchard had stopped for gas. "Go on," Chris said, handing me some change. "Call your grandmother."

* * *

The phone in our apartment rang for a long time before

I decided T.J. must still be in the hospital. I was surprised when, after I asked for her room, the switchboard operator at St. Mary's said, "One moment, please." So T.J. kept the phone.

Rita picked up, another surprise. She sounded excited, and that wasn't a surprise, just depressing.

"I'm taking T.J. to Mexico. Soon as they release her. We're going down to Juarez where it's nice and warm and we can get treatment for her."

"You're what?" On the other side of the road a barn had caved in years before. Still visible was a ghostly gray advertisement for Red Man chewing tobacco, an Indian chief under a huge wreath of feathers. I was only half listening to Rita. T.J. would never go to Mexico with her—at least, not until the universe shifted on its axis.

"You've heard of it?"

"Heard of what?"

"Laetrile."

It sounded familiar. Then I remembered. It had been in the newspapers. "The cancer cure from apricot pits?"

"Right."

"That's quack medicine," I said. But then my heart stopped. "T.J. has cancer?"

"No. But if it cures cancer, think of the other benefits it can give."

I rubbed my face. "Can she talk?"

After a moment I heard T.J.'s gruff voice. "I'm getting out of here tomorrow. Where are you?"

"I'm in New Orleans. I've been in jail. Didn't you get my letter?"

"I thought you got out of the joint a couple of weeks ago." I noticed she was breathing heavily.

"I did get out. And then I got arrested a second time."

"Were you doing anything more interesting than sitting on a bench?"

"I think you must be better," I said. "At least you're feisty again."

"Say listen, talk your mother into going to Mexico by herself, would you? I'm not up for another forty-eight hours of her delightful company."

"Is she still there?"

"No. She went down to the cafeteria to get me some pomegranate juice. Of course, they don't have any pomegranate juice in the cafeteria but that doesn't stop her. She goes down every day to get some. So when you coming home, or is that classified information?"

"I'm not sure. Soon. They taking good care of you?"

"What is it you have to do out there, Jeri—what's so all-fired important?"

"I'm trying to save a man's life."

"Of course," she said dryly. "But I think you need to back off, missy. You're riding that white horse right into the ground. Time to give the poor nag a rest."

"I'll be back in a few days. Love you."

"Yeah, I can tell," she said. And the phone went dead.

* * *

"She can't stay." Paul herded Chris and me into a separate room, away from a small group meeting around a table. "You know that. This is what comes from you encouraging her."

"I couldn't let her go up there alone, Paul. Be realistic."

"She'd better get realistic. She needs to be on the first plane back."

"I'm not going to do that."

"You don't have a choice."

"Oh, yes, I do." I turned and started for the door.

"You see?" Paul said to Chris. "Just like I told you, a loose canon."

"Jeri. Please."

"If CORE won't help me, I'll sleep on the street. But I'm going to find out what Ellis Lee did before I go back to L.A."

"If you sleep on the street, you'll be arrested," said Paul.

"Good. Then I can tell the papers how CORE wouldn't help me save a black man's life."

Paul clenched his jaw. "I had a feeling about you. I should've kicked you out when I had the chance." He came around me and shut the door. "Sit down. We've got to talk."

"I don't have to talk to you, Paul. You're not my boss."

Chris said, "Sit down, Jeri. Please."

I shrugged. "I can listen standing up. Say what you have to say."

Paul leaned against the edge of a table. "Okay," he said. "That threat about the press is ridiculous. They're not going to give a rat's derriere about Ellis Lee."

"Well, that's where you're wrong, Paul. Because a New Orleans reporter already investigated Ellis's case."

Chris rolled his eyes but Paul didn't see it.

"Would you tell me what you think you're going to accomplish here?"

"I'm going to look for the article. When I find it, I'll know what he did. Mr. Starkweather gave me the name of some lawyers in Chicago who will take his case. But I have to know what his crime was supposed to be."

"If you find the article, then will you go home?"

"Of course."

"There's nothing 'of course' about you, Jeri. I want your word. And this time I want you to keep it. I'll give you three days—"

"Five."

"Four days. Then, come hell or high water, you're on a plane and gone. Will you give me your word?"

I raised my right hand. "Girl Scout's honor."

"This isn't a joke."

"I'm not joking. I promise. Four days. Then I leave."

* * *

A small well-dressed black man opened the front door. We greeted him with that fake cheeriness people put on when they feel like they're imposing but have no choice. I'd asked Chris if we couldn't rent a room, but he said staying in the community was part of building the Movement.

Mr. Washington showed us through a narrow hallway into a living room crammed with furniture and reeking of chemical lemon. The three of us filled up the room. He called upstairs and a woman came down, her hair wrapped in a checkered bandana. She sat in the one chair, leaving Mr. Washington to squeeze in next to us on the sofa.

"Y'all is welcome to what we has. There be a small room upstairs and you can sleep in there," she said to me.

"Thank you."

"I'm sorry to say we haven't got a bed to offer you," she told Chris. "This couch have to do, I'm afraid."

I turned and looked at him. His skin was gray. His ribs had to be killing him and the thought of him trying to sleep on that small couch stirred all my feelings of guilt. If I'd gone home, he could have had the bed upstairs. But Chris only said, "That's fine, Mrs. Washington. I appreciate it."

In the bedroom, she smoothed an imaginary wrinkle in the chintz bedspread. "Y'all come down here to try 'n make things better. This seem like the least we can do. Let me get you some towels. The bed's fresh changed, so don't be worrying about that."

Standing close to the window screen, listening to bugs banging into it, I took several deep breaths, trying to solidify into the person Mrs. Washington had made up this bed for. I removed my shoes and lay down on the spread, telling myself I'd take a bath in just a minute.

When I woke up, sun leaked through the cracks in the shade covering the window. Mrs. Washington must've thoughtfully lowered it when she came back with the towels she'd placed on the foot of the bed. I burrowed under the pillow and groaned. Chris tapped at the door and told me to get up.

I sniffed my armpits. They were fetid. I opened my suitcase and pawed through my clothes. Most were soiled. I thought it might be best if I stayed in that room forever, avoiding the company of cleaner, better-looking people. But I needed to use the toilet. The house was quiet. In the bathroom I found a note from Chris, saying he'd already gone and telling me which bus to take to get to the downtown library.

I stood with the note in my hand, wishing he'd sent me a note like this in the workhouse. Wishing I knew where he'd been all those days.

* * *

A pretty, bored-looking young woman boarded the bus and came to the back. She wore a starched blue and white uniform and "Pauline" was embroidered over her pocket. Our eyes met briefly, hers widened slightly, and she looked away.

Through the window I spotted a cluster of black men waiting under the gray suede sky, squinting up at the possibility of more rain. A station wagon pulled up near them and the men flexed their muscles. One had an open crate filled with rocks at his feet. He lifted it as if it weighed nothing, but the muscles in his neck and arms bulged. He held it away from himself and swung it left and right, his eyes on the station wagon for signs of interest. He must've been too old because a much younger man with a broad chest, massive fists slashing air, was beckoned into the backseat by the driver, a white man with sausage knuckles coiled around the steering wheel. The young man sat with his head pressed to the window. I think he liked being chauffeured. Half of a grin showed on his face as the station wagon passed the bus.

A lame black woman dragged her bad foot up the sidewalk. She wore several layers of clothing. Under her arms seams gapped, allowing other broken seams to spill through like stuffing. As the bus inched along in traffic, she gained on it, pausing every few steps to raise her hand as if she were waving hello to the driver.

When she climbed up, I turned toward the window and listened to the Morse code of her bum leg being pulled along the aisle. My nostrils filled with the reek of wet wool, and the seat beside me sank down. I eased slightly away from her. Sooty grey fingers clamped the rail before us. In her lap was a stained cloth bag, fading chartreuse flowers stitched into the grimy burlap.

Her rheumy eyes scratched at my face and I turned unwillingly toward her. "This here's a nigguh seat."

"It's—it's all right," I stammered. I looked around. The bus didn't seem to be segregated. A black kid sat near the driver and another dark-skinned man sat three seats away from the kid. We hadn't reached the library, but I tried to get up. "Excuse me," I said, hoping to squeeze past her spindly legs without fracturing them.

She sniffed. "The back's for nigguhs. Y'all gets the whole front part to y'selves."

I stood round as a question mark over her knees. The bus

driver's eyes met mine in his mirror. He started to close the doors and I sagged back toward the seat. Abruptly she swung her legs into the aisle so I was able to scramble free. From the street I looked up and saw she hadn't moved from the aisle seat. She sat there staring down at me. As our eyes connected, her lips curled.

The rain broke just as I reached the steps of the library, drenching me before I could get inside. For a few minutes I stood just inside the door, watching water pelt the street. Then I squared my shoulders and went in to begin the search.

The index revealed nothing. Ellis Lee was not mentioned. "Are you certain that's his full name?" the librarian asked me, and I realized with a shock that I was not certain at all. "Well," she sighed, "I expect your only alternative is to look through the microfilm itself. Not everything would be in the index."

I cranked the first page onto a small screen and turned the focus knob until the blurred squiggles solidified into headlines. The small print was harder, but with concentration, I could read it. Fidel Castro marched into Havana and declared Cuba free of General Fulgencio Batista. On the editorial page a columnist named Ryberg examined what he called *nuclear paranoia*. He said that the first cavemen to stumble onto a way to make fire were probably equally frightened. Reading this brought back memories from the fifties of curling up under my school desk, wondering if a pair of hands knotted over the back of my neck would be enough to keep me safe from an atom bomb.

I moved through the pages slowly, afraid Ellis Lee's name would appear and be gone, just four lines—although if that reporter followed through, there should be more of a story.

Joe McCarthy was memorialized again two years after his death. A woman threw acid in her sleeping husband's face. Several school districts were considering ways of circumventing the 1954 Supreme Court ruling on segregated classrooms. After hours at the microfilm machine, I hadn't gotten through three months.

Chris touched my elbow, and I let out an involuntary squeak. "I thought you might be ready to take a break by now."

"Has the rain stopped?"

"Sure. How'd you like to do some sitting-in?"

"Is that the kind of break you're referring to?"

"You have a choice. You could picket."

My shoulders ached. "I can't take the time, Chris."

"Let me tell you a secret about microfilm. The longer you stare at it, the more bleary-eyed you get. Eventually you get so punchy, someone could place a sardine dead center on the screen and you'd keep reading around it."

"'Well, I'm not there yet. I've only done three lousy months."

"I bet you're reading. That's it, isn't it? You're reading."

"I have to read. Otherwise I'm going to miss it. I'm sure they didn't give him the front page."

"You're an amateur. Here, watch a professional in action." He took the three reels to the desk and requested three more. I noted the pained grimace when he lowered himself into the chair. "Now, follow the leader," he told me. "Just like Papa Tomato said when he put his foot down on Baby Tomato: Catch up."

He cranked so the pages flew past. "You won't find him in the women's section," he pointed out reasonably enough, whipping through them. "Don't tell me you've been reading about debutantes and brides?"

"Just some stuff about how to clean a stove with a toothpick."

"Get busy." Within less than an hour, between us we'd gone through six more months.

He shook his head. "Nothing."

"We could've missed it, we were going so fast."

"We didn't miss it. But what you need right now is fresh air and a picket sign. Follow me."

Outside the sky was the color of the blue ribbons T.J. used to tie in my hair. It felt good to be out, but I couldn't stop thinking about my deadline. "There must be a faster way to do this."

"Another day or two—as long as you resist the temptation to read—if it's there, you'll find it. Otherwise, there's nothing more you can do, Jer. You know, even if you could get him a lawyer, you'd wind up doing more waiting. Every court victory means more waiting. That's why these guys are on death row so many years."

"Not in Mississippi," I said. "Those people don't dawdle. Less than a year, gavel to gas chamber. In his last State of the State speech, Ross Barnett boasted of their efficiency."

23

I ASKED the librarian for the next three months of microfilm. Today, I was going to find Ellis Lee. Without fail.

But after half an hour of turning the crank, my spirits drooped. I'd never find him. And I couldn't stop reading. The United Nations chastised Israel for the Palestinians. A baby was burned in her crib by a boyfriend seeking to punish her mother. The mother was reported hospitalized "in shock." A reader expressed appreciation for the editorial decision to try publishing a special "good news" edition of the paper.

The "good news" issue told of a man who had come back to his family after nine years, having fled because he couldn't support them, but returning to find he'd inherited his father's business with enough money to send all five children to college. A group of teenaged girls planned to bring Easter to shut-ins, delivering baskets filled with homemade breads, preserves, and candies. The pages were drenched in this sort of sugary news. The incinerated baby had depressed me but somehow all that cheerfulness made me sadder. Monday, sixty-nine children slaughtered by police at Sharpeville, Tuesday, pretty girls delivering home baked goodies to housebound grandmothers—tra la tra la. It was as if the paper had done a front page spread on Nero fiddling and buried the bit about Rome in ashes.

But turning the knob past *Good News Tuesday,* I found a small blurb about a black man arrested for murder in southern Mississippi. I sat up straighter, my heart beginning to thrum, but his name turned out to be Orion Yates and a few issues later he hanged himself, or the paper said he hanged himself. I liked the sound of Orion's name and wrote it several times, maybe just to christen the—to that moment, blank—notebook.

I felt a physical need to see Ellis Lee's name on the screen, but the microfilm rolled by, page after page, giving me nothing. At one point, I woke from a stupor. How long had I sat blindly staring? I glanced around, half-expecting to see Ned or Dorothy or even Thomasine sneering at me. What had she told Sweet Pea? That I was crazy? It did seem crazy to be sitting there, getting nowhere.

When I came blinking into the glare and heat at closing time, I spotted Chris. He said, "Want to walk back together?"

I slid down to the steps, exhausted. I hadn't eaten. "This is pointless," I told him. "I think I have to go to the newspaper."

"It's closed."

"Newspapers don't close."

"The part you want does close. You can go tomorrow." He pulled me to my feet, but in his face I could see how much the gesture cost him. "I keep forgetting I shouldn't do stuff like that," he said with a pained smile.

"Should we sit down again?"

"Not a good idea. Let's walk." Heat rose from the sidewalk and I thought of Dasante Mitchell saying, "You could fry an egg." Much hotter, the rubber soles of my sneakers would melt. We'd gone about three blocks, Chris holding his side, when he said, "Listen, Jeri, we're going door to door tomorrow morning and we need more bodies."

If the sidewalk made me think of Dasante's speech, this tapped into its most powerful moment. I was in the church on Sixth Street and Dasante was telling me the Movement needed bodies and then he was pulling me onto the dais and thanking me for answering the call. In my case, the call had gone unanswered for too long, but I couldn't take the time. "I only have two more days."

"If the newspaper can find that article for you, it won't take them two days to do it. In the meantime, you owe the Movement some effort, don't you think?"

I chewed on my knuckle. "If I come, will you go to the paper with me tomorrow afternoon?"

"Sure, why not?"

Except for his ribs, he seemed practically serene, all the awful things he'd spat at me while we were sitting on the floor of Reverend Carroll's car vanished from his mind. But those accusations were thorns in my memory, and I couldn't keep from wondering: *Where were you? All those days in the workhouse, where were you?*

24

DOROTHY SAT DOWN next to me in the meeting room. She was wearing a beige dress that sagged on her stick body. I was surprised to see her.

"What's wrong?" I said. "You look upset."

Up front, Paul and Chris were arguing about how many blocks each person should cover with the leaflets. "It's not a hit and run," Paul was saying. "We want to spend some time talking to the community."

Dorothy said, "When are you going back to L.A?"

"Paul didn't tell you?"

"Tell me what?"

"I'm here on sufferance. He gave me four days. Day after tomorrow I have to get out of town."

"I'm sorry to hear that."

"Really?"

"I've never been your enemy, Jeri."

"Come on. You don't like me and you know it."

"That's not true. You made me angry. That's not the same

thing as not liking you."

"It sure felt the same. Hey, don't sweat it, Dorothy. I've been disliked by experts."

She rubbed her hands as if they were cold. "I came to apologize."

"Apologize? For what?"

Paul clapped for attention. "Okay. Let's talk about what to say out there. Everybody come on up front."

Dorothy didn't move. "Ellis Lee," she said. "I didn't give you enough credit." She pulled out that lace handkerchief and blew her nose. "I heard about the workhouse."

"Dorothy! Jeri! Front and center."

I stood up. "Who told you?"

Dorothy didn't move. "My husband. He thinks quite a bit of you." Her smile was lopsided and bitter. Crimson mottled the whites of her eyes. "I'm sorry I didn't give you credit for being the serious person you are."

"C'mon, Jeri! Dorothy!"

"Well, I said what I came to say." She got up. I put a hand on her arm.

"What's wrong, Dorothy?" She looked down, and didn't answer.

A young boy brought us a stack of leaflets. She waved him off.

I grabbed some flyers and went after her as she started for the door. "Wait a minute—"

She shook her head.

"Jeri, we're waiting. Maybe you and Dorothy can have your little chat later?"

"All right, Paul. Just a second." I went to her and spoke in a low voice. "Is it your husband? Is he all right?"

She shook her head again, and fled.

I moved to the front of the room. Paul was already giving

instructions but he stopped briefly to say, "So nice of you to join us."

"What happened with Dorothy's husband?" I asked him.

"Nothing," he said. "Far as I know."

* * *

An oily film coated the sky and there was a pregnant heaviness to the air. "I hope this isn't tornado weather," said Chris.

"When I was a kid, I wanted to be blown into another dimension, just like Dorothy in the *Wizard of Oz*. But you know L.A. No chance of that."

"We turn to the left up ahead."

The street was no longer paved, just dirt that would turn to mud when the sky emptied its reservoirs.

Chris said, "So what happened with Dorothy? Why'd she take off?"

"She's upset. Something about her husband. Do you know him?"

"Only from Parchman. He wasn't a very friendly guy."

"He doesn't exactly write mushy love letters to his wife either," I said. "You should've read the note he sent her in Parchman. I've seen warmer greetings on a PG&E bill. She was positive he was dying. I thought she was losing her mind. And then he writes *I'm fine* and doesn't even bother to sign his name."

"It's a male thing," said Chris. "We're a naturally taciturn species."

"Is that why you never told me why I didn't see you in the workhouse for a week? 'Cause you're the strong silent type?"

His jaw stiffened. "I thought we were talking about David."

CANDIDA PUGH

"I thought we were talking about men." He made a face.
"Fine. Let's drop it," I said. "So, tell me, was David the one
who fainted in the hole?"

"Hell no." Chris looked sheepish. "That was me. I made
it through three hours but I passed out when they opened the
door. It was a bitch. If I wanted to scratch my nose, it took
ten minutes to work my hand up to my face. Turn here. Our
territory starts on the next block."

We turned into a narrow alley with no sidewalks. The
houses were grimy boxes, too makeshift even to be called
shacks. Most of the windows were covered by a piece of
cardboard. The richest families had tin patches on their
windows. Children played in the street, with no toys beyond
one slightly deflated basketball.

"I'll take the next block, you take this one."

"I thought we'd be working together. I don't know what
to tell people."

"Well, I guess you should've come up front and listened
to Paul instead of gossiping with Dorothy. Read the flyer."

He sauntered off, leaving me facing cardboard windows
and swollen plywood doors. I leaned against a light pole and
read the flyer. It urged people to stop shopping downtown.
Did CORE imagine people in this neighborhood ever went
downtown to shop?

At the first house I tapped softly, half-afraid of shattering
the door. From behind a screen, rusted into honeycomb,
a woman's face peered out. "You there!" she bawled and I
jumped back.

The flimsy door flew open, almost knocking me over,
and she glared into the street. She was wearing a cotton shift
that could have been stitched from flour sacks. A naked baby
clung to her shoulder.

"You there! Jerome! Don't you try 'n hide from me, boy!

207

You stop that, hear! Just stop that! Don't you go messing with that child no more or I be coming upside your head!"

A small boy said, "Yes, ma'am."

She glanced at me and I held out a leaflet, but she didn't take it. I tried to explain the boycott but she stepped back behind the screen, shaking her head. Then she closed the door.

Some people were rude, some elaborately polite, but nobody seemed interested. I explained we were trying to end segregation downtown but I might as well have said we wanted to turn all the shops on Canal Street into candied apples. A few people tried to make me keep the leaflet. "Ain't gonna read it noways, no need to waste it."

There were scattered tin cans around, licked clean by dogs. Wads of toilet tissue teased into the air by warm gusts of wind. I stuffed leaflets into mailboxes or under doors when no one answered my knock. I wondered if Chris was having any more luck than I was.

A fat, cheerful baby looked at me from the road, squatting at the bottom of three rickety steps. I grinned at him and his moon face split in a smile. Dark brown slobber oozed between his small, white teeth. I could smell it before I got to him and spotted the cigar-shape he gripped in his chubby hand. I slapped it away and picked him up, holding him as far from me as I could without dropping him, praying his face wouldn't touch mine.

I screeched, "Hey! Whose baby is this? Someone!"

A man opened the door at the top of the steps. He was well over six feet tall and dark as a moonless night, only the whites of his eyes and an occasional flash of snowy tooth breaking the density of his face. He wore an unbuttoned blue work shirt and Levis and he stood barefoot, studying me. I saw a resemblance to the child.

"What you be doing with my baby?" he asked mildly. From behind him the half-light of a television flickered, the only illumination in the room. A very pregnant woman sat with her profile toward me.

"He was down there," I said, pointing to the patch of dirt. The man looked dutifully at the spot I'd pointed to, and nodded. "He had a—dog—turd."

"Is that a fact?" He looked at his baby as if noticing something to appreciate that he hadn't seen before. "What you be doing with something like that, boy?"

The baby reached out, gurgling happily, but his father made no move toward him. I thrust the child at him. "He was eating it."

"No," said the man, taking his son.

"Yes."

"Well, Ma'am, I do thank you kindly for troubling with him and I am sorry you had to witness such a horrible thing, I truly am."

"The dog could be infected. He could have parasites. Anything. I mean, your baby needs to be looked at. By a doctor."

"Ma'am?"

I was struck by the careful way he rolled ma'am around his tongue. "Maybe a clinic or something."

"I expects he'll be all right." He put the child down. "Run to Mama. You all nasty, Michael." The boy toddled inside to his mother. Dust particles swarmed around her as she rocked slightly in her chair. "I hopes he ain't ruint your dinner, ma'am."

"Willie," whined the mother, "come get this baby off'a me. Making so much racket a person can't hear nothing. And he stink too."

"This here lady say Michael been eating dog do."

209

"Phew! No wonder he smell so bad."

The little boy hung across his mother's shallow lap, stabbing the floor with his naked toes. I looked at him, sadly envisioning what I saw as his life, and then I turned toward his father. Our gazes held together, softly, intimately, almost erotically. For just one second, I thought we might have a conversation that wasn't poisoned. Then he said, "If there ain't nothing else, ma'am. I surely do thank you for taking the time to bring this to our attention."

I started back down the broken steps. "Hey, wait a minute!" I yelled, remembering the reason I was in that alley. The door, in the midst of closing, wavered and then squeaked open again to reveal the still smiling man. He listened politely to my spiel and took the leaflet, elaborately folding it, saying, "My, my," his eyes sparkling with amusement. Again he said, "Thank you kindly," and, "We do appreciate it." I heard the click of the door latch.

As I moved away, I pictured him cleaning his child's dog-shit-smeared hand with the flyer I'd just given him.

* * *

When I was a child, there were moments T.J. had looked at me with pinpoints of rage in her pupils, and I could half-sense her rooting around in her conscience for justification. Maybe years before, bitterness had germinated from her struggles to be a woman alone when women were not supposed to be alone, when women were not expected to struggle. But I had other memories. She sat beside me at the kitchen table, my small dark head bent stubbornly against her help.

In her worn work clothes, her elbows coming through as she leaned over my schoolwork, she'd be saying, "We'll learn this stuff together." And she had learned it, racing on ahead of me, staying up reading half the night while I slept. Ready the next day to explain the math problem, to answer questions about the book I'd read and not understood.

But my opportunities must've had a downside for her, she must have envied me a child's life much richer than anything she had experienced. My whining about classmates with Pendleton jackets and crew neck sweaters, penny loafers from Bass, and real pearl necklaces—it all had to have galled her, recalling that boy in the dirt with his head kicked in, recalling the nun bulldozing her way into their privacy in search of too much food, driving her father out of T.J.'s young life—her mother, ancient at forty, dead at fifty.

Did that black father, looking at my white face, feel some of what T.J. had felt? Did he despise me because I couldn't appreciate the privileges that allowed me, with leaflets in my hands, to step into his privacy?

* * *

Chris was beaming. For the first time since that day at LeCharles's house, he seemed to move without wincing. "What happened, Jeri? Your leaflets are soaked."

"So am I, but, hey, first thing's first." He glanced at me, looking puzzled. I started walking. "How come *you're* dry?"

"A guy invited me in. We had a long talk," he said, hurrying to catch up. His breath turned ragged, and I felt a stab of guilt and slowed down. "He might picket with us this afternoon."

"Yeah? Great. I caught a kid eating dog crap and everybody who came to the door looked at me as if I was from Mars. Most wouldn't even take the flyer." I tossed the soggy leaflets into an open garbage can next to Smoky's Laundromat. Inside, a young brown-skinned woman hunched over an infant, feeding him a bottle under a poster of another brown-skinned woman giving another baby a bottle of Similac. "Anyway, who is at

CORE that's crazy enough to think people around here shop downtown?"

"These people may be poor, Jeri, but they have to shop." Chris smiled. "C'mon, let's go get some lunch. You'll feel better. Then we'll head over to the *Clarion*, what do you say?"

"I don't have money for lunch."

"Forget it. It's my treat."

I felt my lower lip jut out and I could almost hear T.J. say, "Be careful, Jeri. Your face is going to freeze like that."

"I can't be sponging off you all the time."

"We're talking about a buck-fifty, tops, and look at you. And you need to eat. You're wasting away."

I couldn't figure out why I felt so cranky. Maybe it was that neighborhood, all those people living so miserably. Or maybe it was just that they didn't like me. I did feel a pang of jealousy over Chris getting that guy to invite him in when no one would talk to me. I was beginning to believe I couldn't do anything right.

We found a diner a few blocks away. The black cook looked at us hard before he came over with two plastic glasses of water. Chris handed him a flyer and asked him to tape it up in his window.

"Y'all ain't boycotting me, is you?"

Chris laughed and ordered two Cokes and two grilled cheese sandwiches. "I'm keyed up," he said when the cook went back to his grill. "This guy's a fantastic find. He's in the janitor's union so we can use him to reach a lot more Negroes."

"If he shows up."

He arched an eyebrow. "You really are in a bad mood today," he said, taking a pill vial from his shirt pocket. He shook out two tablets. "For the pain."

"Yeah, I know." I knew it was wrong, but I took his broken ribs personally—the pills, the wincing, his hand finding its way to his side. Every reminder inflicted a little razor slash of blame, as if he broke out in an agonized sweat now and then just to punish me.

A heavyset woman came in. She sat at the back, making no effort to hide the fact that she was staring at us. I gave her a sarcastic wave. Chris glanced over. "Who's she?"

"I don't know. Maybe she works for the cops."

The sandwiches and Cokes arrived. "What's bothering you, Jeri?"

I shoved my plate away. "The same thing that's been bothering me ever since we got out of the workhouse."

Chris paused, the sandwich near his mouth. He put it down.

"Where were you?" He took out a cigarette and lit it. "I keep asking but you won't answer and I don't know why."

Something stirred in his eyes. He blew smoke toward the window. "The warden gave me a job in his office."

I was shocked. "You worked for the warden? Doing what?"

He grimaced. "Writing reports for the State Bureau of Prisons."

"Reports? About the prisoners?"

"It's not like that," he said, putting the tip of his cigarette into the ashtray.

"No? What's it like?"

"It's just numbers."

I tried to take all this in. "Why didn't I see you in the dining hall?"

He picked up his sandwich again, but I could tell his appetite was gone. It was just something to put between us. Even so, he took a bite and chewed deliberately. Finally, he swallowed and said, "I ate with the guards."

"Jesus." I looked over at the staring woman. She seemed benign now, concentrating on a plate of French fries. "I—I thought they killed you, I felt it was all my fault—you *said* it was my fault." I put my head in my hands. Without looking at him, I said, "Didn't you wonder if I was okay?"

"You were with the Negro women. I knew you had to be a lot safer than I would've been with the white men. How was I to know you'd pick a fight with a lunatic?"

"Pick a fight? Are you serious?"

"I apologize. That was out of line. But, look, I begged you to let it go but you keep hammering and hammering. And now you don't like what you're hearing. That's why I didn't want to get into this, Jeri. I knew you'd act like this."

Soggy bits of paper had blown up against the window. "I don't understand, Chris. You ate with the guards—but only for a week?"

He looked at his sandwich. "One of them complained. And since the report was finished—" He shrugged. "The warden didn't need me anymore."

The view out the window was bleak, windswept newspapers plastering paint-chipped walls. Across the street stood a boarded-up barbershop with a *For Lease* sign on the door. The candy-striped pole leaned against the wall, much of it reduced to twinkling chips of glass salting the sidewalk. "Well. I guess I better get going."

"You want'a wait for me?"

I hung the strap of my purse over my shoulder and thought, *Good job, Jeri. He's not happy now.* I started to put my hand across the table, to say, *never mind, it's okay.* I owed him so much. And it was my fault the deputy kicked in his ribs. But I couldn't get away from the feeling that Chris had betrayed me. All the sweetness of the things he'd done drained away.

As I left, the table held two sandwiches, one with a single bite out of it and the other untouched. Chris was lighting another cigarette.

25

AT *THE CLARION*, six or seven people, sitting at desks behind the counter, held telephones to their ears. A woman with wildly disordered red hair and pale bluish skin greeted me with a toothy smile. She never looked directly at me, but always slightly above my head or over my shoulder, turning around several times to glare at a ringing phone no one answered.

"We don't do that," she said. "The thing is, we don't have the personnel. And research takes so much time."

Chris had said it wouldn't take days to find the story. But it seemed they wouldn't even try. "I thought you'd have some kind of index."

She chuckled. "You must think we're the *New York Times*. There ain't no way we could keep up an index. Not if you don't even have the date—I mean, at least the year, sugar."

"But surely there must be somebody here who could take a quick look through two or three years. A man's life depends on my finding that article."

"I'm sorry. But looks like you're gonna have to find some other way to save that nigger, honey." Another telephone began jangling. "I should get that," she said, looking just above my head.

"Who's in charge of the archives?" said Chris. I turned around, startled. He stood in the doorway.

"That would be Miss Downey, but she's out sick. I expect she'll be in tomorrow or the next day and she can tell y'all how long it might take her. I mean, if she wants to, but no one else here has the time."

Chris said, "Tell Miss Downey we'll be back tomorrow."

We stood on the sidewalk outside the *Clarion* office. "I'm useless. I can't even give out a lousy flyer, but I think I can save a man's life. What a joke." A group of white teenagers hurled past us, laughing. "What if that woman doesn't show up tomorrow?"

"Then we'll come back the day after tomorrow." I flashed him a disgusted look. He knew I had to leave. "I'll talk to Paul."

"It'll be a waste of your breath. He wants to be rid of me. Today was probably the capper for him."

"He doesn't like it when people don't pay attention."

I passed my hand over my face. It all seemed so pointless. Chris stood apart from me, looking on edge. "I'm going back to the library. I don't know what else to do."

He checked his watch. "I promised to meet Paul at two."

"Yeah, fine," I said. "Go."

He hesitated, patting his pocket as if he were searching for a cigarette, but when he found the pack, he dropped his hand and just stood there, looking dejected.

People around us turned into blurs. "You blamed me," I said, as if we had been in the middle of talking about the workhouse instead of Ellis Lee's future. "Just like when you told Paul what I was going to do. You didn't have a right. You made me think I could trust you and then you turned against me."

"Yeah, well, I'm not perfect."

I blew my nose and jammed the used tissue back in my purse. Then I waved my hand vaguely because I couldn't speak, except to mutter, "Yeah. See you later." A bus swung around the corner, coming within a few feet of me, and Chris yanked me back to the curb. For a moment, he held onto my arm and I swayed toward him.

Then he let go.

* * *

I sat down at the machine and began again, but I couldn't concentrate. I read a few of the crime items, even though I could see right away they weren't about Ellis Lee. A man was accused of murdering and dismembering his nine-year-old daughter. He'd taken out a life insurance policy on her two weeks before her death, but since the policy specified that she had to be dead and since the dismembered corpse had been hidden over fifteen miles of terrain, the father had been unable to collect. This blundering on his part bothered me almost as much as the murder itself. She died for nothing. Several issues later, the father claimed his innocence, that he'd loved his child, that he had his own suspicions about the guilty party. No one expressed much interest in his suspicions, not even the newspaper. Eventually he was sentenced to die. There was a picture of him in the paper, taken the day of his sentencing. He looked so ordinary, I felt sick. I got up and went into the restroom. While I was cooling my face against the mirror, I remembered I hadn't called T.J.

* * *

I went into the hallway and found a pay phone. As I dialed her apartment, I wondered how my grandmother had managed to hold onto it. Maybe she hadn't. Who would've paid the rent while she was in the hospital? Not Rita, I knew that much. But, to my relief, T.J. picked up on the second ring.

"How are you?"

"How the hell do you think I am? You planning on coming home any time?"

"Day after tomorrow. I see you still have the apartment."

"Hells bells, course I have it."

"I was afraid you might lose it while you were in the hospital."

"I got disability, Jeri. But it's great you thought I was homeless and you stayed down there."

"Don't give me a hard time, please, T.J. I wanted to come home."

"What? You hadn't finished patching up the South? Los Angeles wants to know when you plan to get around to fixing it."

"I'm glad to hear you're okay. You were in the hospital a long time."

"Those doctors were just running up the bill."

"I hope you're taking good care of yourself, Grandma."

"Where the hell did *Grandma* come from? You never call me *Grandma*."

"I just—you know—I love you."

"Listen up, Jeri. Nobody's making funeral arrangements so don't go counting your inheritance before I croak."

I said, "Yeah, yeah, yeah." She guffawed but said nothing

more, just hung up the phone.

* * *

Dorothy stood on the library steps. "Find anything?"

I shook my head. "How'd you know I was here?"

"Chris."

"Oh." She looked as if she expected something. "Why'd you come looking for me, Dorothy?"

She shifted the strap on her purse. "No special reason. I wanted to see how you were getting along, that's all."

"Well, I'm not getting along at all. So I'm going down to the canal for a breath of fresh air." She looked so forlorn, I hesitated. "What's wrong?" She didn't answer, but I couldn't make myself walk away and leave her there. "Want to come with me?"

When we got to the canal, she sat down on a low wall. Standing next to her, I squinted out at the MAYAN, a blue and white vessel with smoke stacks puffing and a sprinkling of tiny men at the rail.

"What're you going to do now? I mean, about Ellis Lee."

I took my sunglasses off and cleaned them with my shirt. I felt drained, no longer even sad—just emptied out. "I don't know." I didn't want to tell her about *The Clarion*. Some superstitious impulse made me feel if I described my last hope, it would evaporate.

"He left me."

I frowned. "Who?"

"My husband. David."

"Oh, jeez." I put my glasses back on. "I am sorry."

Her smile quivered and she lifted her hand to her hair, but it hung there, as if she'd forgotten what to do with it. "He's giving me a very generous settlement."

"David has money?"

"His family gave us a big wedding—the Beverly Wilshire. Do you know it?"

"Heard of it."

"The waitresses were all in black taffeta. Very elegant. It was the first—and last—time I tasted caviar. I had to spit it into my napkin. David's mother said, 'This is the worst I ever ate.'" Tears coursed down her cheeks. "I thought she liked me." A soft breeze rose up and the air freshened a little. Dorothy wiped her face. "I asked her to lunch at the Wilshire on our first anniversary. She was busy, of course."

I fanned myself with my hand. Why was she telling me this? Didn't she have a friend to talk to? Maybe not in New Orleans, but why didn't she go home?

"My mother wore black. The mother of the bride. In mourning." She laughed harshly. "Now it seems appropriate. At any rate, it was the only nice dress she owned. I told her David would buy her another one but she was too proud. So naturally people kept telling her to bring out more hors d'oeuvres. And she'd go to the kitchen and get them. Even the help at the Wilshire thought she was one of them." Dorothy slumped, her body jagged and awkward, a woman who could never bring herself to round her shoulders. "I told her not to do that—she was embarrassing me. But my mother never could bear to hurt anyone's feelings."

It crossed my mind that her mother could bear to hurt Dorothy's feelings.

Five students wearing red and blue school jackets came toward us, shoving each other and laughing. They glanced over and I tensed up. But they passed on without a word. I don't think Dorothy even saw them.

"You know when I knew I'd lost him, Jeri? It was when I watched you read the note he sent me."

"That was a mean note." I shaded my eyes and focused on the haunches of the MAYAN as it slipped away. *In a month*, I thought, *I'll be eighteen. And Ellis Lee will be dead.* I couldn't remember exactly how old he was. It seemed monstrous to me, that I should forget his age before he died. All I knew was that he'd had a birthday on Friday the 13th. "We should get going."

She looked up at me, her face gray. "David had a vasectomy before we got married. Did you know that?"

"What's a vasectomy?"

Her smile was small, secretive. "I wonder if his girlfriend knows about it."

"David has a girlfriend?" I sat down.

She sniffed, wiped her nose, and threw back her head. "He didn't tell me about the surgery. He'd volunteered for a study, said he was contributing to medical science. David's always contributing." I thought she might have meant this sarcastically but she didn't sound sarcastic. It seemed she still thought of him as a great man.

The MAYAN released three dismal bleats and joined a line of ships making a blurred streak as the sky beyond them deepened to red. A small, dark blue vein cut across Dorothy's temple. There was something regal about it.

She wrapped her arms around her shoulders. "How can a woman sleep next to a man and not know?"

"Do you want to start back, Dorothy? I don't think it's possible, but you look like you're getting cold."

She shook her head, dropping her hands into her lap. "If he'd been dying of cancer, I wouldn't have noticed. That's what he said." She looked down at her long slender fingers as if they might be strangers she didn't want to meet. "He waited five years for me to notice."

"David's been having an affair for five years?"

"But he's right. He's not blaming me, he's just trying to help me understand how—how he drifted away. Of course, I'm angry," she said, as if I'd argued with her, but I couldn't see any anger in her. "But I can't blame him. David never hid anything. All the signs were there. I was the one who chose not to read them. All that time, he was simply waiting for me to be ready for the truth." A baby bubble of snot ballooned out of one nostril and she pressed her handkerchief to it.

Something came to me then, an awful thought, but I couldn't close my mouth on the question. "Is she white?"

Dorothy crumpled, her face contorted, sobs wracking her bony frame. I reached over and gathered up that broken woman, and we sat for a long time with our arms around each other, long after the sun had melted down into the water.

26

EARLY THE NEXT morning Chris knocked on my door.

"Can I talk to you?"

"You want me to come downstairs?" I said. "There's not a lot of room in here."

"This will only take a few minutes."

"If you're going to apologize—"

"Yeah," he said. "I want to."

I shook my head. "Don't worry about it. Doesn't matter."

"Yeah, it does. I was up most of the night, thinking about what I did."

I scratched a swelling on my arm where a mosquito had gotten me. "You risked your life for me, Chris. I don't have a right to be mad at you."

"I didn't earn a free pass."

"Okay, then. Apology accepted." I stood there, waiting for him to nod and go. But he didn't move. "I mean it, Chris.

224

I'm over it. Mostly."

"There's something else."

"Yeah?"

He looked at his feet. "I was—you know—I was, uh, with someone—in a relationship. It started when I was a freshman in high school."

"Sheila mentioned it."

He looked awkward, standing in the hall, his hands seeking some place to steady themselves.

"Why don't you come in? We can sit on the bed."

He perched on the edge of the mattress, looking out of place with all that chintz. I pulled my legs up and crossed them, facing him.

"I told Sheila my girlfriend left me because of the Freedom Rides, but that wasn't it."

"Before you say anything more—I want you to know, I understand what you did. Because of your ribs. You couldn't take a chance. It was the right thing to do, Chris."

"But that's not why you got upset. I figured out that much."

"Yeah. Funny. You accused me because you didn't want me to find out the truth. And I got mad at you because you accused me of something I knew was true. I *was* the one to blame for what happened to you."

"You're pretty headstrong, all right. But I've stopped looking to blame anyone."

"Maybe you could still blame the Marivale sheriff."

He rubbed at the chintz. "Yeah. Well."

"So you want to tell me why your girlfriend really broke up with you? Or maybe you don't want to talk about it."

"Oh no. I came up here to talk about it. Well, I mean, I came up to—" He sighed. "This is hard."

"You don't have to—"

"No, no. I have to." He sat for a long moment, his head hanging, looking like a little boy made to stand in the corner. "We were in Chinatown. Eating dinner. And there was a blast. Huge. I never felt anything like that in my life. I mean, my body felt like it was exploding. When I came to my senses, I was half a block away." He ran his hands over his hair. "I just fled. I didn't even know I'd done it."

"What about your girlfriend? Was she hurt?"

He shook his head. "When I stumbled back to the restaurant, she threw her engagement ring in my face." He rubbed his knees. "Some kind of gas explosion in the kitchen of a restaurant two doors down. Blew out a lot of glass but that was about it—except for that kitchen." A fly hummed behind the shade. "She called me a coward."

Muscles in his face twitched and I saw the effort he was making not to break down. "You believed you acted like a coward at Marivale, taking that job. Is that right?"

"Something like that."

"Listen to me, Chris, you're not a coward. You've been incredibly brave. Over and over. And you've been a good friend to me, from the beginning. With a couple of minor lapses," I said, smiling. "Right from when you sat next to me on the plane. Nobody else wanted to."

"I only sat with you because I thought you were cute."

"Yeah, I must've been adorable, puking my guts out. But you were right, you know. We're not perfect, either one of us. Still, I have to admit, between the two of us—I get the imperfection trophy. I've messed up everything I've touched ever since I got down here."

"I don't know about that." He rubbed his cheek. "If today doesn't—well, if it doesn't go the way you hope—if you need to stay, Jeri, I can help you do that. CORE doesn't have to be involved. I can find you a room."

I shook my head. "Uh uh, but thanks anyway. I'm going to beat my head against this one last brick wall and if it doesn't give, I'm going to do what everybody's been telling me to do from the beginning—even Ellis Lee."

"Well, if you're sure that's what you want."

"What I want is to find out Ellis was framed and the Chicago lawyers will take his case and they'll get his conviction overturned and we'll all live happily ever after."

* * *

I stood in the open doorway, hesitating, when the harried redhead called out, "Hey, shut that door! You're letting flies and heat in here."

"Is Miss Downey here today?"

The redhead impatiently motioned me to come inside. "I remember you. You and that good-looking young man come in here yesterday. Miss Downey's in the back. I told her all about that handsome boyfriend of yours."

"And Ellis Lee—?"

"Yeah, I told her about the nigger. Hold on. Sit down over there and I'll bring her out soon as I finish with these copies."

I perched on a wooden bench and set my pocketbook in my lap. I probably looked like a high school kid waiting for her prom date. Except, of course, I was wearing a skirt more creased than Methuselah's face.

A woman in thick glasses rimmed in ice white came out and looked vaguely around. She had jabbed several bobby pins into her short, gray hair to keep it off her neck, causing clumps of it to fan upward. The effect was comical, but I was a long way from laughing.

"The only thing I can think is it must've been one of them Good News Days," she said. "You know, some lady wrote in with the idea, all about how people get tired of reading so much depressing news and couldn't we at least now and then put out a paper with nothing in it but good news. The editor, Mr. Winkle, thought it was a real nice idea, and Mr. McIvey, the publisher, was away on a long holiday, so he didn't know anything about it until he got back. He fired Mr. Winkle, said the man ought to go be a fry cook if he didn't know any better than to put out a newspaper that didn't give anybody any news. If your nigger done his killing on a Good News Day, that would explain it."

My skin felt icy. "Explain what?"

"There ain't a thing in the archives. Miss Ralston told me about it this morning—I come in at six—and I looked all through them, couldn't find one word about it."

The morning light coming through the venetian blinds flickered. "Nothing?"

She looked at me hard. "Are you all right?"

"I've looked so long. So many places. It seems I would've come up with something by now if there was any fairness in the world."

"It might never have made the papers, you know. Not every killing does."

"But maybe it wasn't a killing. I mean, it doesn't have to be murder, does it? Doesn't Mississippi execute people for other things?"

She came up to the counter. "You look kind'a peaked like," she said. T.J.'s word. "Maybe you better sit down. I'll fetch you a cup of water. Go on. Sit over there."

I found my way back to the bench and dropped down onto it. Miss Downey came through a swinging gate with a paper cup. "Drink this," she said, placing my hand around it. "Drink it down now."

I took a sip. It was ice cold and made my teeth ache.

"They won't take the case if I don't know. I can't do anything if I don't know."

"Finish the water. It'll do you a world of good."

"When they told me a reporter had gone to Colfax, I thought, that has to be it. The people at *The Clarion* will know what happened."

"What reporter in Colfax?" she said, tilting her spraying head. She looked like a graying rooster. "'Cause, honey, I bet I know who that is. We don't send too many reporters over to Mississippi. That had to be Nelson Eddy."

"The singer?"

She chuckled. "Our Nelson Eddy's a reporter. What's called a stringer. Well, I don't think he's a stringer anymore. Did Nelson get put on regular?" She turned to Miss Ralston.

"He has his own column. You ought'a know that."

"Oh, yes. Well," she tittered, "I don't read them. I just archive them. Is Mr. Eddy here today?"

"I'll call upstairs and see," said Miss Ralston. A moment later she said, "He said he's coming down here to see you."

"Okay," I said. Was this it? "Okay," I repeated. "Good."

I waited fifteen sluggish minutes, my eyes fixed on the clock above Miss Ralston's desk as it tapped out every second. Sometimes I thought Miss Ralston and Miss Downey must be toying with me. Could there be a reporter named Nelson Eddy? And could it be that after all this time, I'd found the man who investigated Ellis Lee's case? Then I'd think, no, they wouldn't toy with me. For all their talk of "nigger," they were kind women, kind to me anyway, even though they knew I was on a mission to save a black man. I remembered telling the cop in the Jackson Police Station I didn't understand him, that he must be speaking some ignorant local dialect. I was closer to the truth than I knew. These women didn't even realize the cruelty of what they said. Like my mother. *Nigger* was just another word to them.

Was it possible Nelson Eddy was waiting for me to go away, that he didn't want to talk about Ellis Lee, just as nobody else wanted to talk to me about him? But that couldn't be what was keeping him from coming downstairs. He probably didn't even know what I was there to see him about. Miss Ralston had been on the telephone only a second or two.

"You wanted to see me?" His wrists poked out of the sleeves of a cheap blue cotton jacket and his tan pants were what T.J. called high-water pants, sloshing around his bony ankles. I could have grabbed his jug ears and kissed him.

"You're Nelson Eddy?" I stood up and gave him my hand. "I'd like to talk to you about Ellis Lee."

His eyes went blank and my stomach did a flip-flop. "Who?"

I started to cry.

"Who are you?"

"Jeri Turner," I sniffed. "I thought you were the reporter who went to Colfax, Mississippi looking for the brother of Ellis Lee who's on death row at Parchman."

He took my elbow. "There's a coffee shop next door. Let's go over and get a cup."

I gathered up my purse with shaky hands and followed him out the door.

He didn't say another word until two cups of coffee were placed on the table.

"Milk?" said the waitress.

Nelson Eddy stirred the milk into his cup far longer than necessary. "What do you know about Ellis Lee?"

"I know he's supposed to die in two weeks."

"How do you know about him?"

"I was a Freedom Rider."

"You were at the Farm?" I nodded. "How'd you make

contact with Lee?"

"We talked through a vent. He was in the cell behind mine."

Nelson nodded and took a sip. The coffee must've burned his mouth because he put it down fast. "So what is it you want from me?"

"You went to Colfax? You talked to his family?"

His eyes grew dreamy. They were pale blue and the lids above them were a slightly paler blue. "I wanted to do a human interest piece. The making of a criminal, stuff like that."

"The making of a what?"

"I wasn't sure the paper could use it, but the editor told me to go ahead and see what I could find out."

"What did you find out?"

"Not much. Did you go up there?" I nodded again. "Then you know. They don't take kindly to white folks from out of town. The sheriff practically ran me out on a rail. I think only my down home accent kept me from being thrown in the clink."

"I can testify to that."

"He put you in jail?"

"He did." I played with the sticky stainless steel napkin holder. "So, tell me. Please. What did he do?"

"You don't know?"

"That's why I'm here. Nobody will tell me."

"I don't wonder. It's not a pretty story." He tried the coffee again, blowing on it softly. When he'd settled his cup back down, he said, "Ellis Lee was in for a robbery. He's not a real bright fellow. Held up a hardware store in Tupelo. Used a little toy gun. Guy at the counter laughed him out of the store but they picked him up outside and put him in Parchman."

"They put him on death row for a toy gun?"

Nelson signaled to the waitress. "I'll take one of them

jelly donuts, if you don't mind, Nancy. You want one?" I shook my head. "Just one then, that's a good girl." He stirred the coffee some more, blew on a spoonful of it, and sucked the spoon dry. "He escaped. Him and another fella. Broke into a house about ten miles from the Farm. Old lady lived there alone. She was blind, half crippled up. Her son comes by and does for her, but most times she'd be on her own. Independent type. Those boys raped her and stole what little money she had. I think they took away twenty-six dollars and change."

The room swayed. "Maybe she had it wrong. You said she was blind."

"She knew their voices." The waitress placed a sugary bun in front of Nelson. He bit into it and jelly spurted onto his plate. "You thought he was a good 'un, huh?"

I looked at the purple-red splotch and swallowed bile. "I did."

"Maybe he got religion. Folks say he could be mean."

"He was never mean to me."

"You gotta believe it's a different man's gonna face death."

"Maybe he's being framed?"

"Case looked solid to me. Son came home, Ellis Lee and the other one took off out the back. Son called the police. They picked those boys up just a few blocks away from her house. Had her money and her steak knives in their pockets."

"What were they doing with her knives?"

He shrugged. "Probably thought they could stab the dogs, if dogs were sent after them."

"But why? Why did they go to her house?"

"Rumors she had a lot of money stashed away. I'll say this for them, they didn't beat her. But I think they might've said they was going to rape her just to scare her into telling them about the money. Things just got out of hand 'cause there wasn't any money to be had. She's just a poor old widow lady, living on public assistance. Sad thing is, colored people around there say she's always been good to them. She couldn't see, so probably the color of somebody's skin didn't matter to her a whole lot."

I wiped my eyes and blew my nose. "What am I going to do?"

"Why do you have to do anything?"

"I said I'd help him. I said I'd get a lawyer."

He dabbed at the purple smears around his mouth and put the crumpled napkin into his plate. Signaling the waitress for the check, he said, "Jeri, it's not my place to tell you what to think but maybe you should let it go and focus on what y'all came South for in the first place."

He placed two dollars on the table and I reached for my purse. "This one's on me," he said, waving me off. "Especially as you didn't touch your coffee and didn't want a donut." He stood up. "I've got to get back. Why don't you sit here and drink that coffee? You look like you could use a little time to pull yourself together."

I did sit there. The clock made a full circle before I felt strong enough to stand up and go to the door.

"Y'all come back now, hear?" called the waitress. I gave her a feeble wave and went out.

* * *

When Chris came in, I was sitting on the Washingtons' living room sofa. I don't know how long I'd been sitting there, dimly registering the sounds of traffic, footsteps, the creaking of old boards. The feeling I might be sick had passed hours before but I hadn't eaten anything. I kept seeing a glob of purple jam on a white plate.

He sat down and put his arm around me. "No happily

ever after, I guess?"

"The Chicago lawyers said they'd look into his case."

Chris dropped his arm. "Well, that's good, isn't it? Does it mean he's innocent?"

I thought of the *Good News Day* paper that held nothing of value. "It's rape. It looks like he's guilty."

He fingered the ashtray, nodding. "She's white, of course. The victim."

I tugged on a loose thread in the sofa cushion. "I've been sitting here thinking I don't know how many Negro women have been raped by white men. I'm pretty sure none of them ever got punished for it, not around here."

"But you can see why Pelton and what's his name from the NAACP—Logan—you can see why they didn't want anything to do with this guy."

"No, I can't see that, I'm sorry. Why didn't they?"

"It's like with Rosa Parks. They picked her because she had a spotless character. There were others who could've refused to give up their seat, but the newspapers would've had a field day with them. The first woman they were going to use turned out to be pregnant and unmarried."

"But, hey, it's okay for you and me not to be perfect," I said. "Isn't that what we said?"

"We're talking about distracting attention from the central issue. It's all about PR, Jeri. Public relations. You can't hang a movement on a bad guy, even when he's getting a raw deal. And it doesn't sound as if Ellis Lee's getting that raw a deal. Rape's a serious crime, even when you're a Negro."

"I can't believe you're saying that."

"What? That rape's a serious crime?"

"No. That—that you can absolve Mississippi because, what the hell, he did it. A crime he'd get away with if he was white and she was black. But, the hell with it, let them kill him."

"That's not exactly what I said."

"It sounded like it to me."

"People make their own beds. Ellis Lee knew the stakes when he committed rape. Unless he was retarded, he knew where he was living."

"You? You're going to talk to me about somebody exercising personal responsibility? Then how come you put your mother's suicide on your father, huh? What's her personal responsibility for that?"

"That's a low blow, Jeri."

"Maybe it is. And maybe you need to think about it anyway."

"Maybe I do, but it's none of your business." We glared at each other but I looked away first.

"You're right. It not my business." I started to stand up, but he put a hand on my arm.

"Don't go. I'm sorry I snapped at you. That's just—it's hard for me to hear that."

"I know. It's all mixed up in my head too. I mean, there's T.J., needing me, and I'm responsible for her, but I'm here, probably on a wild goose chase. That lawyer didn't give me a whole lot of hope."

He nodded. "So. When do you go?"

"Tomorrow at 10."

"You saw Paul?"

"I don't think he believed I would leave until I asked him for the ticket."

"Did you tell him about Ellis Lee?"

I shook my head. "He didn't ask. But that's okay. He was in a hurry to see me out the door. I seem to have that effect on men."

Chris looked at the table, a slow smile dimpling his

cheek. "You know, ever since I watched them haul you out of that police station, shrieking, 'Now I am a Communist!'— what can I say, Jeri? You've scared the hell out of me."

"See what I mean? I bet you're going to be glad to see the back of me too."

"I do like that view," he grinned. "The truth is, I've never known anybody like you."

"Hey, y'all." Mrs. Washington slammed the front door.

Chris called out, too loud for that tiny house, "I got a roasted chicken for dinner, Mrs. W. It's on the sink."

"Ain't that nice?" She came to the living room doorway, carrying a sack of groceries. "I can make us something real good to go with it." She turned and went into the kitchen.

I said, "I better go give her a hand."

* * *

At the airport, Chris walked with me to the gate. "I'll call you when I get back to L.A. But don't look for me too soon. I'm going to Mississippi to register voters."

"Just don't go near Colfax."

"What're they going to do? Kill me? Oh, wait. They might." He chuckled. "What're your plans for when you get back, Jer?"

"Get a crummy job. Probably join CORE. Bring the fight home, the way T.J. wanted me to. I hope Paul hasn't had me blackballed."

"I saw him last night—after you went to bed, he came over to say goodbye. He was sorry to miss you."

"I bet." A truck pulled up alongside the plane out on the tarmac. "He was probably checking to see if I'd packed."

"He said you have a lot of spunk. He admires that."

"Oh, right. I'm sure."

Chris shrugged. "So. How's your grandma?"

"I haven't talked to her since the day before yesterday, but she was her old self, cantankerous as ever."

A man and woman with a young baby arranged themselves on the chairs nearby. I wondered why they didn't glare at us. Then I realized it was because Chris and I were the same color.

"Scared?"

"It's a lot scarier to demonstrate in Mississippi than it is in L.A."

"I meant about the plane. I won't be there to hold your barf bag."

"You won't be there. Period." Our eyes held momentarily.

"So this is it," he said.

My smile felt tight and artificial.

"Oh, I forgot to tell you. I sent LeCharles a couple of hundred bucks to fix his house."

"Oh, Chris! I'm so glad you did that. I'll pay you back." My voice was husky. "When I can. Which might be never, the way things look. I wasn't exactly earning a bundle at my last job, and I don't think they're going to give me a sterling recommendation."

"Go to school, Jeri."

"You know, I think I will. How does Geraldine Turner, Esquire, sound to you?"

"Attorney at Law? You?" He shook his head. "I'd hate to be on the other side of the courtroom from you. But it's good. It's great. So, you think you'll be okay?"

I looked again at the plane, trying to call up the terror I'd had two months earlier. Had it been only two months? "Maybe I take myself more lightly. I don't see me bringing down the plane this time."

He was playing with the change in his pocket and I

remembered Paul at that first orientation meeting. "I spoke with my dad last night."

"You what? How'd it go?"

He pursed his lips. "Okay, I guess." He jingled the coins again. "No. It was good. He—he cried."

"You mean from happiness, I presume."

"From happiness." He turned those glass blue eyes on me. "You were right, Jeri. What you said yesterday—I talked to him about it. It turns out he tried a lot harder than I ever knew—you know, to try to keep her from killing herself."

The loudspeaker blared, *Now boarding at gate 44, American flight 808 to Los Angeles*. I rummaged in my purse for my ticket. When I found it, I pretended to keep searching. I was trying to keep from bawling in front of him.

Chris reached out and chucked me on my chin, muttering in a bad impersonation of Humphrey Bogart in *Casablanca*, "Remember this, kiddo. We'll always have Colfax."

"Very funny," I said, wiping my eyes. "Please come home in one piece, Chris."

"I'll do my darndest." He handed me something. "In a few years, Jeri, you're going to make some man miserably happy, I'm sure of that." He moved closer and wrapped his arms around me, and I hugged him back very gently.

Then he took my face between his hands and kissed me, a long sweet kiss. "Stranger things have happened," he murmured into my hair. "Could be you already know the guy."

* * *

As I strapped myself into my seat, I looked toward the terminal and saw Chris through the window, waving goodbye. I lifted my hand to wave back, even though I was sure he couldn't see me. That's when I noticed he'd put something in my hand just before I ran to the gate. I had *To Kill a Mockingbird* back. And then I remembered him calling out, "Look inside," and wondering what that meant, assuming it meant I should look inside myself. But as the plane taxied down the runway, I opened the book and there was Chris's inscription:

Dearest Jeri,

Like you, Atticus is a giant killer. Like you, he ran into a giant he couldn't kill. Let him tell you about it on your journey back across the bridge of the single hair.

Love, Chris